THE MARKHOR
SPORT IN CASHMERE

THE MARKHOR
SPORT IN CASHMERE

HANS VON KÖNIGSMARCK

GYAN

Published by

Gyan Publishing House
5, Ansari Road
Daryaganj, New Delhi-110002
Phone: 011-47034999, 9811692060
E-mail: books@gyanbooks.com

Distribution Network
gyanbooks.com
India, USA, Canada, UK, Australia

ISBN: 978-93-7169-333-2 (PB)

First Published, 1910

2nd Impression 2025

Printed at: Gyan Press, Delhi.

THE MARKHOR SPORT IN CASHMERE
Author: HANS VON KÖNIGSMARCK

[*Frontispiece.*

THE MARKHOR.

THE MARKHOR

SPORT IN CASHMERE

BY

COUNT HANS VON KOENIGSMARCK

MAJOR ON THE GERMAN GENERAL STAFF

AUTHOR OF "JAPAN AND THE JAPANESE,"
"A GERMAN STAFF OFFICER IN INDIA," ETC., ETC.

TRANSLATED FROM THE GERMAN
BY
NORAH BASHFORD

LONDON
KEGAN PAUL, TRENCH, TRÜBNER, & CO., LTD.
DRYDEN HOUSE, GERRARD STREET, W.
1910

DEDICATED

TO MY AUNT AND UNCLE

PRINCE AND PRINCESS OTTO ZU SAYN-WITTGENSTEIN-BERLEBURG

IN MEMORY OF MANY HAPPY DAYS SPENT

AT EGERN AM TEGERNSEE

November 4, 1909

CONTENTS

PART I

IN THE HAPPY VALLEY

PART II

IN THE HIMALAYAS

PART III

IN THE REALMS OF THE MARKHOR

LIST OF ILLUSTRATIONS

TRIGLAVROSES *

By the stream stands Anka in all her pride,
Young Janez climbs down the mountain-side;
A chamois rests on his shoulders broad,
He waves his hat trimmed with tassel and cord
And a bunch of Alpine roses.

With a laugh proud Anka gives him her hand:
"Hast brought me ought from the far-off land?
What! nought but pinks and the gentian-bell,
And edelweiss and the blue speedwell?
And not one Triglavrose?"

Young Janez says, with a shake of the head:
"The Triglavrose is the flow'r of the dead!
From Zlatarog, blood of the chamois wild,
Doth spring the bloom thou long'st for, child,
The crimson Triglavrose.

"The huntsman, who sees from far away
The chamois' golden horns, must stay
His foot, for never may he dare
To glance at the white nun's paradise fair
Which Zlatarog doth shelter.

* An extract translated from Rudolf Baumbach's poem, "Zlatarog."

"And whosoe'er the chamois slays,
The forfeit dear with his life he pays—
Sweet Anka, light of my eyes, thy slave
Will do thy bidding: ask all things save—
The crimson Triglavrose."

Proud Anka pouted her lips so red:
"A fig for thy Zlatarog," she said:
"A man of courage, with me as his bride,
Should laugh at the white nun's angry pride.
Go, fetch me Triglavroses!

"Go, bring me the roses as I say:
So much for my kisses thou must pay!
Janez, good night, good night, good night!"
Proud Anka calls, and runs from sight;
And upward climbs young Janez.

By the stream stands Anka in all her pride,
And looks through tears at the mountain-side:
"Young Janez, ah! will he never come?
Three days and nights have come and gone
Since he began his climbing."

Proud Anka, hide thy face and weep;
Young Janez is sleeping his last long sleep,
Young Janez lies on the snowy height,
Young Janez holds in his dead hand tight
The crimson Triglavroses.

Many a year hath come and gone,
But Anka stands there still forlorn ;
And if a huntsman passes by,
With a foolish smile she'll beg and cry—
"Go, bring me Triglavroses!"

NORA BASHFORD.

PART I

IN THE HAPPY VALLEY

CHAPTER I

GUEST OF THE 10TH HUSSARS AT RAWAL PINDI

RAWAL PINDI!

"Shall I ever see it again? And, even if I do, what will it be like without my good friends, the Bloods?" It was with this reflection that I took leave of Pindi five years ago.

But I need not have troubled my head about the matter, for Anglo-Indian hospitality does not die out, and this time the 10th Hussars took pity on their German brother-officer. All too soon the shrill whistle "too-ee, too-ee," the signal to start, tore me from their merry company. And now begins a long journey to the mountains in a two-wheeled cart. Oh, those bad springs, those rough roads, those horses that galloped, trotted, shied, stumbled, and reared by turns, that inattention of the driver, and those thousand and one unexpected incidents that occurred —shall I ever forget them?

With several bottles of soda-water and the heartiest of good wishes my British cousins packed me into the mountain cart which rejoices in the name of tonga.

"Better let your servant sit up in front next the driver," said Major Sir John Milbanke, my kind Amphitryon, "then he can at least swallow the dust and any other nice morsels that may fly into the vehicle on this lively drive; also, he will be the first to fall off if the horses stumble or if the wheels come off. Make up your mind to all sorts of pleasant things, especially on the brink of the steepest precipices! Anyhow, try to make yourself as comfortable as possible, for it is an endless journey to Srinagar—three whole days, and up- and down-hill the whole way!"

I sat alone on the back seat and resigned myself to rubbing, pushing, and trying to keep steady by sitting back to back with Paul and the driver. These tongas have a roof curved like a Moorish arch as a sort of protection against sun and rain, and chiefly for carrying the luggage. But it was hard for the latter to withstand the shaking and jolting of the cart, and a good lot of it rolled off into the road when straps and strings could no longer bear the strain.

I held tight with my arms and legs, for the horses started at a sharp trot. Farewell, ye kind and hospitable 10th Hussars!

Not only at every corner, but also on the straight road the tonga-horn blew a shrill note of warning. Run, save yourselves, flee, you pedestrians and oxen-waggons! Room for the tonga!

We left thick clouds of dust behind us as we passed on our way, enveloped in a burning heat. Rawal Pindi in May! It is probably the hottest place in India at this time of the year, perhaps even the hottest in the world!

What a noise! The whip cracked, the horn sounded, the cart rattled, the wheels wobbled, the luggage flew about, the horses' hoofs thundered on. The pace got wilder and wilder, and every minute the heat became more dry and scorching as we rushed on our way towards the Happy Valley.

How few ever reach it behind the high and steep mountains of Life, often so much higher and steeper than the giants of the Himalayas which surround the fertile valley of Cashmere!

CHAPTER II

ON THE WAY TO MURREE

EVERY four miles we have to stop and take fresh horses. "Get ready, get ready," calls the tonga-horn from the distance, and there at the roadside, in the meagre shade afforded by a few dusty trees, stand our fresh relays. The farther we go from Pindi, the smaller, more hackneyed, shabbier, and more waled the poor creatures become. Not until we get to the neighbourhood of Murree and Srinagar do they begin to look bigger and better-fed, and more lively—a tribute to civilisation, which forbids cruelty to animals! Mr Danjhibhoy, the proprietor of this big mail and tonga service between Rawal Pindi and Srinagar, knows his people. He feeds up the thoroughbreds of the towns, and lets them go at a gentle trot through the European quarter. But the time lost by these fine-looking animals on good roads must be made up for by the poor, bony country-breds as they hobble over sticks and stones, hills and valleys. The traveller does not care—all he wants is to get on.

Like so many highwaymen, the lowest of the low, the ostlers rush up to the carriages at each hostelry, tear the horses out of the shafts, drag up the relays, let the heavy pole fall on them, strap the poor things much too tightly, and frighten them by clapping their hands and cracking their whips all the time. It is only with difficulty that the fresh horses can be got to move, and, once started, the pain of their open wounds often forces them to stand still again, and rear beneath the blows of their tormentors. The ostlers standing round come to the driver's aid, swearing, screaming, beating, pushing, until at last, in desperation, the wretched horses start off at a gallop.

Covered with sweat and white foam, with quivering flanks and inflated nostrils, they arrive at the next halting-place. Thus are these poor wretched creatures driven through life from place to place!

What a cruel lot! For ever forwards and yet for ever back again, and the quicker they go forward the quicker must they return to the spot they started from—one everlasting race without a goal, a race unto death!

CHAPTER III

GENERAL SIR JOCELYN WODEHOUSE BECOMES MY HOST AT MURRÈE

OUR road becomes gradually steeper and steeper as we get nearer to the mountains. The poor horses are driven at a hard gallop, and only now and then does their tormentor stop to breathe them.

It is a relief to feel it growing cooler, for even now, after a drive of eight hours, we have reached a height of 6000 feet. Here lies Murree, the big hill-station for the British troops.

All branches of the service on the north-west boundary are gathered together here in the hot season to spend a most peaceful time. Their weapons are balls and clubs! The hottest of conflicts take place on the green lawns and race-courses, on foot, on horseback, with arms, legs, and lungs. Balls of all sorts, from the smallest to the largest, fly through the air, and he who does not himself throw, hit, chuck, kick, knock, fling, or catch, looks on all the more eagerly for his inactivity.

Murree forms an enormous barrackopolis, a gigantic town of tents, during the months of April and June. Military accoutrements parade about with a martial step. The fair sex seem to be in the ascendant—to judge by the hats! And to what an enormous size do the latter grow in this bracing climate! They take the leading place in Murree, strolling proudly through the streets and carrying their triumphs from one playground to the other, only being sometimes thrown into the shade by the flying balls.

Sunset, glowing and fiery, alone has the power to put an end to the game, to banish the most glorious hat, and to call all to rest. After dinner come dancing, theatricals, music, or bridge, or one sits by the fire and fancies oneself at home and talks about coming leave. I am privileged to warm myself for one evening at the friendly hearth of the commanding general, Sir Jocelyn Wodehouse, and Lady Wodehouse, and to admire Armine, their son and heir. Master Armine is an old acquaintance of mine, for he had just been born when, during my last stay in India, I was fortunate enough to enjoy the kind hospitality of his parents.

"The Terrace" is the name of the official residence of the general in command at Murree. I shall never forget the wonderful view one had from here looking towards the towering white peaks of the Himalayas. They seem to be so near, those patriarchs of primeval times, and the more one hurries towards them the farther do they recede into the distance. It is not long before I lose sight of "The Terrace." We go on and on, and our horses become ever thinner.

CHAPTER IV

THE ROAD TO CHACOTI

A FINGER-POST flies past on my right. Too late! We have already passed it! My thoughts only can branch off to Abbotabad.

There, at the present moment, lives one of the best people in the world.

Dear old Lucas, how I should love to have another look at your good, honest, true face! Who is there in Northern India who does not know Major Lucas of the 5th Gourkhas, the general favourite of the Anglo-Indian soldiery?

Suddenly the carriage stops with a jolt. We have got to Kohala, where, in the narrower sense, we now leave British dominions. On the opposite bank of the Jhelum lies Cashmere. A large bridge of modern construction enables us to cross. English iron, iron England, how otherwise should we be able to reach the other side of the rushing stream? All the more proudly do the Cashmere officials collect the road-toll on their side.

"Why twice as much as before?"

"Because the road now becomes worse."

"Will Count Sahib lunch here?" asks Paul. "There is a Dak Bungalow here."

Very soon curry and rice are burning my throat, which I am fortunately able to cool with fruit and little cakes—the kind gifts of Lady Wodehouse. In silence I drink to good old Lucas. "Cheero," was his favourite word as he raised his own glass with a satisfied smile on his true, honest face.

According to orders I sign my name in the visitors' book of the Bungalow—an iron rule as hard to break as the British bridge!

"Curry and rice=8 annas!" How often did these words appear on the same page.

Colonel and Mrs Clifton-Brown and maid had last eaten curry and rice. I wonder who will refresh himself with my leavings?

"Too-ee, too-ee," off we go again towards the mountains, by the banks of the Jhelum, along which it becomes more and more difficult to drive.

"I am determined to reach Uri to-day," I say; "it is said to be the best Dak Bungalow on this road."

"Impossible," answers the tonga-driver, shaking his dirty head.

"General Sahib, Wodehouse Sahib gave orders that we were to get there to-day, so it must be possible."

"Backshish, backshish," I say insinuatingly to

[To face page 12.

PHOTO. HARRISON, FALMOUTH.

MAJOR LUCAS OF THE 5TH GOURKHAS.

the trumpeter of Pindi. He passes on the word, and in the twinkling of an eye the poor, skinny horses are going at a much sharper trot towards the Dak Bungalow.

Long caravans of camels and broad, heavily laden oxen-carts are always getting in our way.

"Backshish, backshish," I cry; but the dull-witted camels and oxen cannot understand, and, in spite of all the tonga-driver's howling and swearing, they refuse to move. We are obliged to drive into them and force our way through in order to get on.

"I insist on getting to Uri," I say doggedly. But I did not succeed in doing so after all, for a landslip had blocked up the road.

"The Count Sahib must pass the night at Chacoti," says Paul, by way of comfort.

CHAPTER V

A DAK BUNGALOW

It was pouring in torrents, thundering and lightening, when at last our wretched drive came to an end before the Dak Bungalow at Chacoti.

"Is there still room?"

"As much as the Sahib desires," answered the butler. "Most travellers go straight on to Uri. There is only one other guest upstairs, and he has just come."

Having delivered himself of this speech, he ceremoniously conducted me inside.

"Can I get anything to eat?"

"Dinner will be served in ten minutes, Sahib."

"What's the menu?"

"Soup."

Of course! There is always some coloured water brewing over the charcoal fire.

"Curry and rice."

Well, that will be a nice change! I haven't eaten that for ages!

"Roast mutton with potatoes and cabbage. Chicken with cabbage and potatoes. Jam-pops."

Bravo! What a splendid menu! I'm particularly looking forward to the pops, which are very old acquaintances. In every bungalow, in every Indian station restaurant, they form the finishing touch to each luxurious meal. Always the same, except that the colour of the jams differs from time to time.

But I must not be ungrateful. In ten minutes the soup, the curry, the rice, the mutton, the chicken, the potatoes, the cabbage, and the pops were all steaming on the table.

Frank Garrett, the other guest, Superintendent of Locomotives on the Rajputana-Malwa line from Ajmere, was my companion at dinner, and we both enjoyed it very much.

Our conversation circled, like the earth, round the sun. "Will it shine again to-morrow? Will the rain leave off and the road be free from impediments?"

The pops were still lying heavy in our insides when the stars began to twinkle, and the next morning we were awakened by the cheerful news that the landslips had been removed.

One rupee, eight annas, was the amount of my bill, and with a good conscience and perfectly abominable pen, I wrote in the margin for special remarks: "Excellently looked after!"

CHAPTER VI

URI

Oh, beautiful Uri, surrounded by snow-giants, bathed in glorious sunshine ! What heavenly peace, for already the last night wave of tourists is rolling on its way to Baramula and Srinagar !

The deserted breakfast-table alone still shows signs of their presence. Alas ! another tonga drives up and deposits a late guest. I share the table-cloth with him and pass him salt and bread. He thanks me with a nod of his head, a very thin, narrow head with swollen eyes that look as if he had borrowed them, and a red nose.

One can't ply a book with questions ; but there is not a single human being who has not some small thing of interest about him, which a discreet question will persuade him to impart—an idea, a well-chosen word, some unusual information, a new way of looking at everyday affairs, or something !

Therefore, out of curiosity, or because I felt bored, I began to talk to my *vis-à-vis*. I asked him where he was going. He made no answer, only looked at me, cast his eyes up to the ceiling, hunted for his handkerchief, and sighed deeply.

"Tell me the story of your life."

His eyes filled with tears, and a deep, pathetic sigh was his only answer.

"Let us be friends; trust me, and tell me all your troubles."

Something rattles in his throat; he chokes, tears roll down his cheeks, he gasps for air.

I make haste to open the window, for the room was really very stuffy and smelt unpleasantly of mutton-fat.

Ah! at last the petrified guest opens his lips, and gives an enormous sneeze.

"Oh, please shut the window. I have a most awful cold!"

"Give me the book, boy. I want to go on at once!" and like lightning I write "Curry and pops," and in the margin for special remarks: "Food bad; everything tasted of mutton-fat, and one guest had a bad cold in his head."

"Very satisfied" was what Colonel and Mrs Clifton-Brown had written just before me. Thus do tastes differ, and according to the cold-in-the-head so is man's opinion of things in general.

I wonder what they are like, these Clifton-Browns, whose curry remains I am always getting dished up? Colonel and Mrs Clifton-Brown! They already seem like old acquaintances to me in this otherwise far-off, foreign country. Shall I ever catch them up, and what will they be like? Let us hope without a cold in the head!

CHAPTER VII

BARAMULA

WE have left the Alps behind us—a long climb, but finished at last—and now here we are suddenly transplanted to that beautiful garden called Cashmere—the Indian Italy, a land breathing of Romeo and Juliet.

We have made our entry at Baramula, where the Jhelum, the Hydaspes of the ancients, leaves its silent, grassy banks to fall headlong into the plains of the Punjaub, becoming ever wilder as it leaps from rock to rock. How quietly it flows here through the valley between its smiling banks! A feeling of warmth and peace steals over our senses. Sweet-scented carpets literally spread themselves out before our astonished eyes—the whole valley is one moving mass of bursting bloom in the June haze. What a sparkling, laughing, enticing world! Nature here draws her resources from the deep wells of life's eternity!

Alas! how quickly the vision fades! We are fast approaching Europe's culture, the great Dak

Bungalow. Here the first house-boats lie at anchor; here are gathered together the caravans of the West. All poetry disappears—the trees leave off their murmuring, the flowers are silent, the waters are heard no more. What shall they do, how make themselves heard, when humanity is making so much noise?

Crowds of brown agents, traders, and beggars welcome me enthusiastically.

They are a mixture of Europe and Cashmere, and in each case the mixture is either too strong or too weak. Like hurrying waves they fall upon the strangers with their hissing sounds of greed, with their arms and with their legs; even the thinnest skeleton does not escape their bloodthirsty croaking, as they pull and tug at him and follow their victim step by step.

No amount of struggling is of any use. Only perfect quiet, complete passivity, and the perseverance of a Buddha, with perhaps a cynical smile or a sarcastic word, will help us, for there is nothing the native hates more than the latter. But make the slightest response, ask a question or give a kindly smile, and you will let loose the wildest elements.

See how they rush and push and wrestle, these Europeanised mountain hordes! They quarrel amongst themselves and underbid each other; each paints the other black, and yet they are all playing the same game. They make solemn asseverations, beseech, implore, and whimper. They praise and puff up every mortal thing: house-boats, servants, shooting, dancers, shikaris, carpets, ibex, preserves, polo-ponies, cigarettes, grass-shoes, picture postcards, climbing sticks, furs, whisky, and bathing-drawers. They pull out the filthiest letters, purporting to be recommendations from the Highest and Most High; they give as references the English Resident, His Royal Highness the Maharajah, Major Wigram, the all-powerful arbitrator of shooting matters, the Vakil Sahib at the Residency, feared on account of his expert knowledge and firmness, and the Lady Sahib, who is still firmer and still more feared. They juggle with princely names, amongst which those of Lily Langtry and Bismarck are not missing.

For the moment they are all well acquainted with the Duke of the Abruzzi, and each of them has been his guide up the K 2, although the Duke himself is still down in the valley. They produce photographs of the loveliest dancing-women and of the most splendid horns of the markhor, the ibex, and bara-singh, with such long antlers that the plates were not big enough to take them. Mercilessly the pack follows me from place to place, until at last, at the gates of the English Residency, they are compelled to leave me in peace. Thanks be to thee, Lady Sahib!

CHAPTER VIII

THE RESIDENCY AT SRINAGAR

THE gates of the Residency close with a snap. Once inside, Asia is left behind and I find myself in an English garden. All around us rise the mountains, stretching their snow-covered heads high up into the heavens. I seem to be enjoying Italy.

The British representative has a regular English house as his residence. The post, at the moment of writing, is filled by Sir Francis Younghusband, the hero of Lhassa, who succeeded in conquering the primeval frozen plains of Central Asia, as well as the Dalai Lama.

Suddenly I find myself face to face with the Lady Sahib, the Resident's wife, who receives me in a manner as gracious as it is dignified. Silently Younghusband offers me his hand. He is a man of few words, but he kindly conducts me to my comfortable room, which smells refreshingly of clean water.

"We are obliged to put you up in the bachelor's quarters," jokes Lady Younghusband later on, and continues to explain in an apologetic voice: "The Duke of the Abruzzi, with his suite, and Colonel and Mrs Clifton-Brown are staying here, and we are rather cramped for room. Unfortunately, too, there is a typhoid epidemic, and my maid is sick unto death, I fear."

Servants in crimson livery hand me tea, etc., and Lady Younghusband sweetens it with interesting remarks about the country and its people.

But she soon leaves it to hurry into a very different land. We wander through the rooms of the Tuileries, through the castles and gardens of Versailles. Sure of her locality, my hostess leads me from spot to spot, enlivening our wanderings with bubbling witticisms, until one fancies one hears the echo of her words from the heart of the Faubourg Saint Germain.

I should have completely forgotten that I was in Cashmere if Indian slaves had not appeared every minute to take orders from their gracious mistress and to carry out her wishes. The aide-de-camp is also flying about with messages, and tells us that the lady's maid is still struggling with death.

But in spite of many interruptions we always return to our muttons, otherwise Louis XVI. and Marie Antoinette, and for a long time we discuss that lovely Queen, whose golden locks turned white in a single night.

But where can Younghusband be all this time?

Official duties had called him away, and I did not see him again till just before dinner.

"Will you take in Mrs Clifton-Brown?"

"I shall be delighted—especially as she has not got a cold in her head," was my mental reservation!

My neighbour on the left was a pleasant American woman, the wife of the well-known Italian physician and mountaineer, Monsieur de Philippi, attached to the Duke of the Abruzzi's suite. She did not, however, intend to climb the K 2, except in thought, and she told me that she should hire a house-boat at Srinagar and remain there in peace whilst her husband made his perilous climb. She also recommended to me a cook whom I shall never forget as long as I live! After dinner I was introduced to Colonel Clifton-Brown. He commands the 12th Lancers in Syalkot, and he brought me greetings from Germany, from the camp at Döberitz, whence he had just returned. In thought we galloped with the Dohna Cavalry Division over the sandy plains of Brandenburg, only to climb at once into the Cashmere hills in search of markhor and barasingh. Later on, Younghusband took the lead and we followed him over the everlasting glaciers of the Himalayas, put the Thibetan general to flight, entered with him the holy places of Lhassa, and looked with wonder at the treasures of the divine Dalai Lama.

How easy all these deeds of valour seemed after a good dinner, and how simply Younghusband told his tale in his almost exaggeratedly modest way!

Really big people never boast. They beautify the temples of the gods, but they themselves remain outside. Thus it is that real talent often works itself to death, whilst little minds loll about on the pillars of success! Even the book of Job *cannot explain* this fact!

CHAPTER IX

THE HAPPY VALLEY

Egern am Tegernsee! but on a much larger scale. A wreath of snow-giants surrounds the valley of Srinagar—the Happy Valley, as the people call it.

The whole of Anglo-India spends its summer here. White maples greet the stranger on his arrival, fields of iris wave their blue and white flags along the edges of the road, whilst gigantic plantains, mulberry trees, deodar pines, and cedars call a welcome.

"Welcome to the Happy Valley, where the world comes to an end and Paradise begins!" India's loveliest jewel casket, full of emeralds and pearls, lying at the foot of the Himalayas, the world's reservoir of rivers and oceans.

Like a green haze the rich vegetation is outlined against the blue in the far distance. The air is soft, bracing, and acts like balsam on the nerves. One can draw deep, refreshing breaths. It is a sweet spot on earth, which causes our souls to expand, and in the depths of our hearts we feel heaven and all its blessings.

Charming miracles and a wealth of colour greet one on every side. The whole valley rings with spring songs ; all the flowers are singing, and everything is bathed in glorious sunshine, from the tiniest meadow flower to the tallest pine. Many a forgotten love-word is whispered in our ear. Joy and exultation seize upon me and almost drown the frolic and rustle, splashing and dripping, chirping and singing, humming and buzzing, sighing and whispering of this heavenly spring-world. Yes! this country is an emblem of heavenly joy. With a feeling of devotion one bathes one's heart and eyes in the clear streams ; with buoyant step one glides over the richly coloured meadows and hurries up the hills to the highest points, where they are lost in the deepest azure—diamonds in the sky. What a fairy-like dream of intangible eternity do these masses of granite, born in primeval times, conjure up!

And it is up there that the markhor, king of the rocks, holds his court. Silvery forts guard his kingdom—a kingdom isolated from the rest of the world. The highest pillars support his throne, and the sky itself is his canopy. Only to the few is it granted to approach him.

Shall I be one of those few ?

CHAPTER X

THE TOWN OF SRINAGAR

WHAT is there to tell of Srinagar, of the actual town itself, where men live? The flowers only blossom on dung-heaps here, and their sweetness makes no impression on one's mind or senses. They romp about in dirty robes on the rubbish-heaps in the streets or on the crooked roofs of time-worn palaces, temples, and sheds.

Even the giant trees of the valley halt before the gates of the town. Only a few willows and poplars, weedy and colourless, make the best of town life on the banks of the canals.

Ever more impassable do the narrow streets become, more twisting, more smelly, dirtier and more Cashmerean, until at last even the giants of the Himalayas can no longer follow us along such narrow paths and byways, where no view is possible. Bent with old age, and as if preparing to fight, the old walls stand opposite to each other, and even shut out the kindly glance of heaven's blue eye. Bursting and rotten they cling together, these perilous walls of a perilous and adventurous time, with their cupolas and minarets, kiosks and arches, halls and cloisters. And they are supported by pillars which themselves require support. Their number is legion. The whole forms one great place of refuge for the people, and over each door hangs a sign showing the date of ruin. All around us are traces of the past, the fragments of the present. Will they survive to-morrow, the day after to-morrow? Probably! For they have threatened to collapse century after century, and yet they are still there. Who can tell whether the new silk factory at Srinagar, a perfect example of the scales and plumb-line, a masterpiece of modern technics in stone and iron, will outlive those crooked old Oriental buildings? So far it has not been possible to draw any such comparison, for this establishment of an industrial centre at Srinagar is the first of its kind in Cashmere, in spite of its being the best-known and most productive silk factory in the world—at least according to Younghusband's last book about Srinagar.

Cashmere is the land *par excellence* of the mulberry tree. And to feed on them, fatten, and spin silk for their new country do the silk-worms come in thousands from Italy and the south of France, their sole reward being a bath in boiling water. It is not long before the fine threads are woven into enormous balls of silk.

Three thousand three hundred men, women, and

children, double as many hands, and ten times as many fingers bring about this wonder.

There is something almost uncanny in the complete power of those thin brown joints, and it is overwhelming to see how they master millions of the finest threads and govern the mechanical action of big wheels and little wheels, cylinders, balls, poles, rolls, innumerable tiny spirals, hooks, teeth, pins, all of which passionately rush, swirl, hiss, roll, squeak, pull, hammer, stamp, beat, whirl, stretch, wind, groan, and tear along under the influence of electricity and Western will.

How much sweating goes to make up those rich brocades, and who would have guessed that so much silk could be spun in this poor State of Cashmere?

It is to Great Britain's spirit of enterprise that all praise is due, and especially to English endurance; for with all their might and main, by all the means possible to their Oriental cunning and obstinacy, did the kings of this district and these mountains set themselves against Western progress. Thus it is that in spite of all persuasion from Calcutta, the many railways planned by the English in Cashmere and Jammu have not yet been built.

Srinagar's silk factory broke the ice of Oriental opposition. It is already the source whence are drawn at least half of the State revenues; it helps the populace to earn honest livings, and increases the well-being of the lower classes. Will His Highness,

Sir Pratap Singh, Honorary General in the English army, be able to stick to his reactionary standpoint in face of these facts?

Up to now the Himalayan giants have been his best allies; they still stand there in their rocky strength and successfully withstand the inrush of Western invaders. But already the wings of English genius are fluttering over the Cashmere heights—already Sir Pratap Singh sees the hills coming nearer—already the waves of the Indian Ocean are beginning to wash the pillars of the Himalayas.

How much longer will the people of Cashmere remain in slave-like ignorance, run about in rags, laughing and playing and pretending, whilst the great ones of the land, born and brought up on the soft couch of riches, carelessly give themselves up to the selfish delights of a luxurious life?

The whole of India is joining in the modern movement towards advancement. Nature's laws demand this, and England's power of colonisation dictates it. Even in Cashmere's future there is a smell of coal.

[To face page 30.

A GOOD BARASINGH SHOT BY JOE PHELPS.

CHAPTER XI

SIR FRANCIS AND LADY YOUNGHUSBAND

I MAKE the acquaintance of the two most important persons in Cashmere—Major Wigram, the demi-god of the shooting, and Mr Peychaud, the head bailiff of the Royal gardens.

Being desirous of shooting a markhor, I make love to the former; but he who prefers roses and good Burgundy had better pay court to the Frenchman. As such he is a favourite of the Lady Sahib. He has to-day presented the members of the Residency with a little gift—a hive full of bees just on the point of swarming. Sir Francis is very fond of bees. I must say I prefer their honey, and I find it considerably sweeter than Mr Peychaud's Burgundy.

Major Wigram is going away on a year's leave, and his divine office is to be filled meanwhile by the ordinary human being, Joe Phelps, a jolly Irishman, beloved of everyone, and not for these twelve months only.

Joe Phelps lays himself out to be especially

useful to the Clifton-Browns and my humble self. Nothing gives him too much trouble: he finds us the best shooting district, provides all necessaries for our house-boat, kitchen and cellar, engages our crew, and for me a shikari, but, thank God! no house-boat. I enjoy that luxury at the expense of my friends. One breakfasts and dines from boat to boat, takes tea on the roofs of the little arks, and glides placidly along with the unconcern of a dead-head.

In all sizes and at all prices these Jhelum yachts are to be had; suitable for bachelors or large families, for American millionaires or British officials of small means; floating cottages, houses and palaces on planks. They can be taken by the week or the month, and one hires the furniture, the cooking utensils, the servants, and the crew all complete, with plenty of worry and annoyance thrown in gratis. Thus do the foreigners in Cashmere float about, roasting in the burning sunshine, travelling in unfavourable weather from place to place, accompanied mercilessly wherever they go by heat, cold, and noisy boatmen—by the English post as well, thank goodness, although the only available address in Cashmere seems to be "c/o The Postmaster, Srinagar." And now, good postmaster, hunt about till you have found the floating or climbing, fishing or shooting, washing or sleeping, laughing or crying, married or single one for whom the letter is intended! For hundreds of these four-cornered boxes are anchored in the river at Srinagar : hundreds find their way down-stream from Islamabad to Baramula, floating about on the canals and lakes, past the three great romantic side valleys, discharging their victims here to-day and there to-morrow.

Wherever Nature beckons, a halt is made, and the unfortunate captain must wander about inland with man and mouse for days at a time, putting up tents, and with the help of the full moon falling into ecstasies and learning to yodel.

Thus does the globe-trotter enjoy Cashmere : the mountains, the water, the trees, the people, and the tinned eatables. Thus does he worship the *dolce far niente*, sleep and dream—all from the Happy Valley ! With enthusiasm he moved in, and with still greater enthusiasm does he move out. Poor Madame di Philippi ! Will she prove the exception to the rule and find peace in her rocking house ?

CHAPTER XII

THE SHALIMAN BAGH GARDENS

THE Happy Valley!

And yet, in spite of this promising name, tales of woe meet me on all sides. My future cook is very ill; Mr Peychaud's bees, including their queen, have turned their backs on the Residency; and the Clifton-Browns have decided to weigh anchor at the end of the week. Thank Heaven, it is only Monday to-day!

"Shaliman Bagh" heads the list of pleasures which Lady Younghusband has planned for to-day. It is really quite touching to see the way in which our kind Amphitryone exerts herself to provide for our amusement—not a day passes that she does not think of something fresh to do or see. "Shaliman Bagh"—the Garden of Love—is situated on the banks of the Dhal Lake amidst scenery of supernatural beauty. What a garden it must be!—one mass of eternal bloom, colour, and loveliness. Here Helen of Troy may remain for ever young, and Romeo and Juliet can never die! Here the great

Moguls came to spend the summer months; here they dreamed away their sweetest honeymoons.

The arrival of the Lady Sahib opens all doors to us, and behind the high walls of the harems we can see the gardens as they rise in great regularity, terrace upon terrace.

But, oh, what a terrible disappointment! All the lovely flowers have been plucked, and nothing but weeds wind their way amongst the weather-beaten mosaics of jasper and porphyry.

Ruins of marble halls, weather-beaten kiosks, crooked statues, broken-down colonnades, crumbling fountains, may remind Lady Younghusband of Versailles; but I, for my part, am disappointed not to hear the drip of water, the pulse of life.

"Shaliman Bagh" belongs to the past. Gone are the pastoral hours when the lovely harem women of the great ones of India played blind-man's buff within its walls, and when Bajadern, hung with glittering garments, pulled the strings of passion, showing their red teeth and dancing with lead in their slippers—painted souls, whose cheeks never dimpled with the sunlight of true happiness—crackling, glistening, sandal-wood flames devoid of real warmth.

And now they are sleeping their last long sleep beneath our feet in company with the emperors and sultanas, whilst we wander about, looking eagerly for what is not here, and finding nothing but weeds, stones, and a dreary stillness.

CHAPTER XIII

FIFTH BRIDGE, SRINAGAR

If, dear reader, you wish to make the acquaintance of the Canale Grande in its most prosaic form, do not go to Venice. Just let yourself be floated down the Jhelum between the walls of the houses of Srinagar. Here you will get a true and unvarnished picture, and here nothing is hidden from the naked eye: neither mankind and his doings, nor the animals, nor the houses. All are exposed to view, and everything is a dirty yellow, except the water, which is black.

As in a kaleidoscope, master-pieces of Oriental life in all its filth and misery pass before our eyes. But only those who have witnessed it in the places of execution at Canton and in the palm gardens of Colombo can form any exact idea of its contrasts. Irises and lilies grow on the roofs, whilst human beings grow up on dung-heaps, and, like the sharp-nosed, four-legged beasts, roll about and sun themselves wherever the filth and dirt lie thickest and form the softest couch!

All the houses are open on the side towards the canal, and the glaring sun draws out and exposes everything mercilessly. One simply has not sufficient hands and fingers to close one's eyes and nose!

It is to the enterprising spirit of Mrs Clifton-Brown and Madame di Philippi that I am indebted for this delightful voyage! They want to buy furs and to take a photograph of the famous Moschee Hamadan. Of course I am delighted to accompany the ladies.

We do not glide over these waters in gondolas. Flat-bottomed wooden boots are driven down-stream by the pestilent water, and six or eight naked rowers row us back later.

We push off beyond the first bridge in the loveliest and greenest part of the European quarter, and the more bridges we pass the more miserable, the more Oriental does the scene become.

At last, thank Heaven! we arrive at the Fifth Bridge, where all the merchants live. Even at some distance off their large signs, with such advertisements as "Lucky Dives," "Poor Lazarus," "Suffering Jew," and so on, can be seen, hung out as they are to attract the attention of the unwary foreigner. My kind hostesses also fall victims to their call, and will not listen to my words of warning, my prayers, and my beseechings! England and America buy the skins of all the animals on the face of the globe, Chinese porcelain, wood-carving, leather and brass articles, and preposterous objects made of papier—or rather "bois"—mâché. They go from Lucky Dives to Poor Lazarus, and end up by making the Suffering Jew happy as well.

One ought never to buy anything at all at these places, for just as the sardines and the curry-powder, so do the most famous Cashmere shawls and other original articles come from Europe, and what is actually made on the premises is shoddy rubbish and not worth buying.

Nevertheless, I did not repent of those long hours of shopping, for they resulted in peace and contentment on all sides—my friends were delighted with their bargains (*sic!*), Lucky Dives had upheld the honour of his house, and even Poor Lazarus was grinning with joy.

CHAPTER XIV

A GARDEN-PARTY AT THE RESIDENCY, SRINAGAR

To-day is Srinagar's big day : the first garden-party at the Residency.

More than a hundred ladies and an equal number of summer gowns are scattered over the English lawns ; the masculine element, on the other hand, being rather thinly represented.

What lyric poetry, what richly coloured gaiety, what *joie de vivre* vibrate to-day through Her Excellency's realms, otherwise so still and exclusive ! What a multi-coloured mass of dresses, hats, fans, sunshades, and flowers—large and small asters, tulips of all colours and shades, dainty violets, brilliant sunflowers, crimson roses, slender white lilies, graceful irises with their astonished blue eyes and fair hyacinth-bells !

Kissed by the golden sunbeams, they all open their petals, whisper many a word of witchery, shoot forth rays of passionate, sensuous colour, these favourites of Nature.

What a rose-coloured reality opens out before us

here—an arena of flowers in which butterflies are fighting, and the more they flutter the more gaudy does the charming picture become!

The sky is so blue, the air is so crisp, the trees shine with joy in their glistening green, and a thousand little green tongues tell each other sweet little stories.

The scent of the roses assails our souls, and we seem to hear the nightingale's loveliest songs, ghost-like, whispering music of the soul, Beelzebub's orchestra. Our nerves are made to vibrate agreeably; one feels the sweet pain of existence, all the joys and torments of love; one suffers and enjoys.

Lady Younghusband, assisted by willing aides-de-camp, surrounded by a flock of red-and-gold-corded satellites, fulfils her office with the skill of a woman of the world and the dignity of the All-powerful One of Cashmere. For each and all she has an agreeable smile, a friendly glance, a gracious nod, a kind word, a little flower or a piece of cake.

Ah, who comes here? No other than the Maharaja in all his glory, attended by his suite. He is dressed in quiet colours, and he does not flutter about, but he is assiduous in his attentions to the Resident's wife and touchingly kind to Eileen, her little eight-year-old daughter. When not thus engaged he looks very serious. A sort of eclipse of the sun seems to rest on his features, and an enormous white turban crowns his care-laden head.

The Royal countenance is of a greyish-yellow hue, and marked with all sorts of queer lines and creases. Sir Pratap Singh is probably thinking of garden parties of the future, when the detested railway will bring still greater crowds to the gatherings. And what will be the good of holding the rank of an English Major-General then?

The Prince very soon takes his departure. As a matter of fact that is all he came for, in spite of his quite palpable respect for the Resident, for Lady Younghusband, and especially for Miss Eileen, whom he pets in a grandfatherly fashion, and than whom he is only the height of his puggree taller.

The Maharaja has gone, but the sun is still shining in all his glory between the heavens and the earth, whilst higher up floats the moon, just a pale little circle. Nevertheless it is enough to warn the guests that it is time to go, and one after the other says good-bye to Her Excellency.

Like a good fairy, but with Imperial dignity, Lady Younghusband presses the hand of each departing guest, graciously smiling, whilst her voice melts harmoniously as she adorns her farewell words with precious stones of flattery. And yet her thoughts are far away from Srinagar, at the court of Louis XVI. She does not see the giants of the Himalayas — she hears nothing but the ghostly, whispering music of the splashing fountains of Versailles.

And meanwhile the garden becomes darker and darker, whilst the moon shines all the more brightly. Like a resounding echo one can hear the last caressing whispers of the flowers and the butterflies as they breathe them into the sweet-scented and flattery-laden air of the silvery night.

Farewell, sweet flowers!

Part II

IN THE HIMALAYAS

CHAPTER XV

FIRST CLIMB BEYOND SRINAGAR

The Egern of India has at last been left behind, with its memories of happy hours—passed all too quickly! Already we have climbed the Indian Wallberg, and bade a last farewell to the town of roses, butterflies, and house-boats!

Srinagar forms but a dark line in a network of silver, and the Dhal Lake glistens like a small mirror. From the distance one could easily mistake it for the Tegernsee, and imagine that one was in dear old Bavaria, with the Wittgenstein Villa lying peacefully in the shade of its venerable lime-trees.

I very soon begin to miss the hospitable Residency, with its gay society, the white poplars, the house-boats, and the flowers; but I try philosophically to console myself with various delicacies which Lady Younghusband, with wise foresight, ordered to be stuffed into my bearers' bags. I can now no longer see the snowy heights which were so plainly visible from Srinagar, whence they seemed so extraordinarily near, for high chains of mountains here shut out all distant views. Like the wings on a stage, they seem to hide the giants in the background in a haze of silver; whilst the Punch, a mighty mountain torrent, hurries down the blue-green slopes, rushing and whirling and hurling itself against the thousand and one islands in its bed, and breaking in whirlpools round black rocks of granite.

It is not long before the traveller finds himself in a tropical wilderness. Lord Weymouth pines, Scotch pines, firs, cedars, wild chestnuts, elms, ash-trees, and maples, with quantities of undergrowth of all kinds, whisper and murmur together. But the thunder of a mighty waterfall drowns all other sounds, and soon we come upon the edge of the gorge which the Punch has hollowed out for itself between the rocks. A thick cloud of foam hides the abyss from sight.

All waterfalls are much the same, but the wild magnificence and intense solitude of the scenery around gives to this cataract a peculiar charm all its own.

One's nostrils are not here offended by the smell of spirits, beer, or tobacco; no visitors' books are to be seen; no picture postcards plague one on every side. There are no climbing tourists here to shout out their drawing-room Tyrolese songs, no Alpine witches to disturb one's peace. Here we have Nature alone in all her grandeur.

And now we have to cross the rushing torrent on a suspension bridge! Involuntarily one wishes, perhaps for the first time in one's life, that one was a tight-rope dancer by trade! Two blocks of granite are united by a rope ladder 200 yards long. I seize a rope and manage somehow, with tremendous swings, to balance myself from one rung to the other. From a height of about ninety feet we have to climb down the rocks to the water below, and, once there, we have the pleasure of going through the same performance in order to get up on the other side. It is with decided inward quaking that I watch my shikaris tumble across in front of me, for they almost seem to touch the seething water at the lowest point. But at last, with a thankful heart, I find myself standing beside them on the further side!

A narrow green valley opens its arms to receive us. Herds of cattle and flocks of sheep and goats are grazing on its sides, and strips of land are sown with millet, barley, oats, and potatoes. Only here and there are buildings to be seen amongst the green.

A few men are awaiting our arrival: models of the Farnesian Hercules, dressed in rags and armed to the teeth, primitive creatures of great strength, and faces full of deep, untutored passions, with hooked noses of a Hebrew type.

Dogs bark out a welcome. The village makes a

homely impression, in spite of its sparse maples and poplars, in its frame of blossoming apple, pear, almond, nut, cherry, peach, and apricot trees. Add to these a wealth of raspberry, strawberry, gooseberry, and red-currant bushes, amidst silvery wreaths of crystal-clear streams, with their green banks covered with red willow-roots, and you have a pretty picture. The yellowish, dirty dwellings disappear in the kind embrace of waving rice-fields, over which flowers of all sorts sprinkle their pretty colours. God made Nature, and mankind the village.

No village of Upper Bavaria this! The human dwellings are gloomy, built of rubble-stones, piled roughly one upon the other, blackened by smoke, grey old barracks, facing the south, and backing on to the hillsides, so that the flat mud roofs run horizontally into the ground behind. During the summer months the cattle are driven into the space thus formed, and a fence on the hillside prevents their getting out.

The roof is used for all and sundry purposes during the daytime. The corn is spread out to dry on it; and here the sheep are shorn, the cows milked, family festivals celebrated, and prayers offered up for the blessing and prosperity of the household at dirt-besprinkled shrines. The family occupies the *bel-étage*—men and women of primitive strength and growth, amongst whom there seems to be a standing bet as to who shall produce the largest family. On the ground floor are situated the winter stalls, manure above and below by way of protection against wind and weather. Round holes in the front walls serve as chimneys, and also provide air and light as far as the smoke will allow.

Layers of filth, collected in the course of years, supply the place of lime and mortar. In the centre of the bare floor is the fire-hole, in which crackles dried cow-dung beneath a sooty pot. This odd firing lies closer at hand than the wood from the hills. Such are the ancestral halls of Cashmere, and thus do their inmates arrange their lives.

They are a dirty people, very dirty, but very friendly towards strangers, kind and polite. They seem to be industrious, modest, and enduring. But they have no Bavarian yodel in their throats; there is no slapping of the thighs in a sprightly dance, nor do they wear the chamois' beard in their hats.

The women of Cashmere are supposed to be specially beautiful—they have this reputation over the whole of India, probably because they have fairer complexions than their sisters in the plains. This is most likely the reason why the big-wigs at the time of the Mongolian rule replenished their harems with Cashmere women. Their children might therefore justly be looked upon as the descendants of emperors!

"Guard your heart against the serpents of Cashmere," runs an old Indian proverb.

But these dangerous beauties are certainly not to be found amongst the fields and mountains. Muscle and bones are here of more importance. And the women hide their neglected bodies in rough garments of homespun linen, the same material serving to make a sort of cap for the head. How artistic these white garments might be if they were not coal-black—black with the filth of ages! Even so they often present a charming picture, these women, when they stand before the dark entrance to their huts with their raiment falling in artistic folds around them—fair silhouettes of Madonna-like grace. But I must not paint them too white, for the nearer one gets, the blacker they become! And then they suddenly veil their emaciated faces and disappear into the smoke-blackened interior of their loveless world.

Poor Cashmere women! Their life is but one long physical and animal existence, knocked about by fate, and only there to serve their husbands and masters—poor shy doves that dare not even coo! Like flowers, kept ever in the dark, they lose their colour and cannot grow, become pale and wither away without happiness! A rugged, harsh existence full of bitterness, which is even discernible in their mountain honey. They never laugh, these mountain flowers, but neither do they know what tears are.

[*To face page* 50.

GENERAL SIR JOCELYN WODEHOUSE AND HIS LITTLE SON ARMINE BEFORE "THE TERRACE" AT MURREE.

CHAPTER XVI

MY LITTLE STAFF HEADED BY PAUL

We had reached Rampur, the last halting-place before beginning the actual ascent. A word from the ruler of Cashmere had put this village at my service, and I found bearers, tents, outfit, and provisions all ready for me.

My little army consisted of twenty-four men. Once again it was Paul Varadara, my faithful old servant and companion on former expeditions, who had seen to the "Bandobast," in plain English, thought of and collected everything that we could possibly want.

Ah, no, I'm mistaken ! not quite everything.

Lady Younghusband's kind thoughtfulness, in the form of butter, milk, vegetables, and fruit, reached me even here ; and my cook, procured after endless trouble, had received his orders direct from Her Excellency. "A term of hard labour in India's glowing plain at the height of summer if I receive the slightest complaint of him," she had added, with a smile.

Three shikaris, the cook, the chiprassi—it was the latter's duty to set up the tents—formed Paul's staff, and eighteen coolies carried the baggage.

The village magnates received me with deference—the Tassildar, the Lambardar, the Jamardar, the Chokidar, the Himaldar, and the Hesseldar. Each of them filled a high office, and they all wore broad, faded ribbons over their rags. I was adorned with chains of flowers and sprinkled with rose-water, whilst expressions of homage were poured out like incense before me, "Uzur qui merbani." "Your honour has only to command," was the chorus uttered by all, accompanied by deep bows and movements of the hand signifying respect: "I will free thy feet from dust, oh, mighty one, and will kiss the ground whereon thou treadest!"

Their faces fascinated me; one could see determination, strength of will, and cruelty beneath the mask of imperturbable calm. I seemed to see a devil in each face; and yet they are children, good children—whether young or old, always children. Education, civilisation have not yet reached these heights; here there are no tigers creeping about, no snakes ever on the watch; the wild creatures in these parts are far more harmless. The tempestuous, plague-stricken plains of India are still too far away to work mischief with word and writ, to stir up hatred against the stranger. Passion is here confined to the village itself; hope and disappointment, hatred and love, envy and the thirst for revenge do not travel much further than from hearth to hearth. Thus no one regarded me as the hated foreigner, but rather as a friend sent by their lord and master, their King over life and death.

The bearers can be seen squatting on their heels in the background, chewing betel-nut and waiting for their burdens. Their faces, disfigured by much hard work and many privations, express indifference and a dull resignation. Six sheep, five white ones and one spotted with red, bleat from time to time: they are to follow as living provisions. There are also twelve hens, with their feet fettered, fluttering about waiting to start—"for laying eggs," as the head of the village was good enough to explain to me with respectful gestures.

"Uzur qui merbani," is the only answer I can get out of all these Secretaries of State of the mountain village to my questions about roads, weather, game, etc.

"And how about the beautiful, rare markhor?" I ask.

"Uzùr qui merbani, very numerous, enormous horns."

"Do you think it possible I shall get a shot at a good buck?"

"Uzur qui merbani!"

CHAPTER XVII

THE DWELLERS IN THE MOUNTAINS

"THE baggage will be sent forward to-morrow morning at four o'clock. The Sahib can follow in the course of the morning. The first camping ground is only twelve miles off."

"Uzur qui merbani" was on the tip of my tongue, but I succeeded in answering correctly, "Very well, Paul."

Sultana, the head shikari, Samdu and Unkar, his satellites, as well as "Mr" Varadara, as the magistrate of Uri called my servant Paul, join me, and the Tassildar, Lambardar, Jamardar, Chokidar, Himaldar, and Hesseldar—the last named was the night-watchman—accompanied by numerous minor lights and by every male in the place, down to the lowest pariah dog, ceremoniously conduct me to the outskirts of the village. "Salaam, Sahib!"—low bows and the waving of hands.

We march on in silence, Sultana and Samdu in front, and Varadara and Unkar bringing up the rear. The ground is still fairly even, the path beaten down by the tread of cattle. A cuckoo calls to us—the first I have heard this year! Have I any money in my pocket to turn for luck?

Timid, white birds, with tails three times as long as their bodies, scurry away before us, reminding one of the mountain women in their hurried, shy behaviour.

Venerable trees spread their giant branches over our heads to shelter us from the glare of the heavens.

By the side of the path is a wretched, broken-down hut, probably the last one in the village, amongst these mountains. Intrepidly I glance within and see the family squatting round the smoking pot: the father, the mother, the grandmother, and the many, many children. Thus they sit all through their lives, only cuddling up closer together as the cold increases.

It is not the inward, mystical power of love, but custom, mutual poverty, an equally low moral standard, and a lack of ambition which hold them together. They scarcely ever speak, and write still less, hence the harmony of their lives.

How different is it with us, where the lives we lead and the way we are educated produce so many differences of character! Each one of us, directly his intelligence is awake, begins to think, feel, and, above all, speak differently from his fellow-creatures. And this is why there are so many misunderstandings, and why one feels so lonely in the crowd.

These dwellers in the mountains breathe as we do, but they know nothing of our world, of the struggle for existence, of ambition, of the stress of work, of tuft-hunting and toadyism. They do not ruminate about the marvels of daylight, nor count the stars in the darkness. They work as long as the sun shines, and sleep as soon as it gets dark. Desire awakes and is satisfied, but further than this their idea of happiness does not go. Farewell, ye simple mountain folk!

With the customary politeness of Cashmere the man accompanies me a few steps from his hut, and then the ascent begins. The path gets more and more uneven. Rampur's civilisation has come to an end. We leave the shadows behind us. The air is filled with a transparent haze. Earth and sky melt into each other on the horizon. We are obliged to wade barefoot through several torrents. Civilisation becomes visibly less, the rocks get barer, the ground rougher, and the angle at which we climb sharper. Snow-tipped peaks begin to appear in the far distance. The sun climbs ever higher. The torrents rush more swiftly on their way—one eternal roar, an everlasting coming and going—the song of perpetual motion. I beg the busy water to bear my greetings on its bosom—to Srinagar, to Egern am Tegernsee!

CHAPTER XVIII

OUR FIRST CAMP

In a circular valley, green and well-wooded, we pitch our tents—three in number. Besides mine there are two for the shikaris, Varadara, the chiprassi, and the cook. Poor unfortunate bearers! they are forced to sleep out in the open. But then they are accustomed to it, in fact, hardly know any other sleeping apartment!

The chiprassi receives me and conducts me to my quarters, where bed, chair, and table bid me welcome. Ram Sheik, too, the cook, soon appears with a steaming chicken. When does the Indian eagle ever leave us in the lurch? The good old sheep is also thoroughly to be depended upon. To-day Murgi, to-morrow Beri. "Skinny, dry, and tough," "tough, dry, and skinny," runs the Indian Vatel's varied menu.

Paul Varadara watches my struggle with the eagle and supports my efforts with Worcester sauce. But I can see nothing but the mountains—so powerful in their nudity!

Sultana approaches, and, with the usual expressions of homage, points to the distance.

"On those rocks over there, there are always good specimens of gorel to be found, good bucks! It is just the old fellows that like to pass their bachelor life there, apart from the common herd. The gorel is very timid and cautious, and only to be found amongst difficult heights."

"What sort of animal is it?"

"A goat," interprets Varadara in answer to my question.

"Is it big?"

"Very big, with good horns."

"But not to be compared with the markhor, I suppose?"

"In Allah's name, no," answers Sultana, in a solemn voice, raising his mountaineer's stick. "Does the Sahib see those rugged cliffs? There I have seen horns the length of my stick!"

Higher and higher climbs the sun in the heavens. Some of my bearers have already bowed to its power, and lie in a deep sleep on the shadeless, burning ground, undisturbed by its fiery rays.

Sleep, thou benefactor of man and beast, Nature's nurse and the brother of death, thou disperser of care and quencher of hunger and thirst, who openest thine arms as lovingly to beggars as to kings, receive me too, a willing victim, into thy embrace!

CHAPTER XIX

RAM SHEIK, THE COOK

PAUL stands at the door of my tent. "Does the Count Sahib wish for tea? It is nearly five o'clock."

"Bring it at once."

"The cook has baked some maize cakes."

"Botheration take the maize cakes!"

I always get into a rage when I think of my *faute de mieux*. Begging your pardon, Madame di Philippi!

And yet he has never done me any harm—on the contrary, he is only too anxious to please me. Is it his face that aggravates me, or his nose, or his two thumbs on the right hand with which he kneads the dough? or what is it? None of my men like him either; they call him "Pakka," the Indian equivalent for "first-class," because he boasts of being the best cook in Srinagar. He calls himself Ram Sheik when he is cooking for Indians, and Anton when he is cooking for Europeans. On the latter occasions he makes a fine show of having been converted to Christianity. Anton is loud, boastful, and officious; Ram Sheik is servile and on the watch, and an exceedingly unsympathetic person as far as I am concerned. And yet I can't say that I dislike his maize cakes.

It is now beginning to get boiling hot in the tent, in spite of the double cover—about 110° Fahrenheit. I drink three cups of tea, and nine, at least, make their way out again through the pores of my skin.

"And yet you are always talking about the cold in these mountains," I say reproachfully to Paul, as he squats in his faithful Hindu fashion behind my chair.

Sultana and Samdu had borrowed my telescope to have a look round after gorel. They return as it begins to get dark.

"What does the master wish for supper?"

"Stupid question! You know as well as I do that it is Beri's turn; but if you can add one of your delicious bread-and-butter puddings, so much the better—only, for Heaven's sake, don't let Ram Sheik put *his* fingers in the pie!"

CHAPTER XX

THE FIRST NIGHT IN THE MOUNTAINS

Sultana and Samdu report having seen some gorel through the telescope. What will to-morrow bring forth?

It is a bright, starry night. Wrapped in a thick coat, I sit before my tent and digest my mutton. All around me fires are glimmering. My men are cooking their evening meal, each according to his caste and faith. Varadara, Ram Sheik, and the chiprassi swear by Brahma at meal-times: their cooking therefore goes on behind a screen. Such is the command of this special deity. A wise law when the menu happens to consist of the best bits from the master's stores! The shikaris are Mahommedans, and do their cooking in public; they also perform their ablutions and say their prayers before meat in the eyes of all men, as the Koran demands of its adherents. The coolies, too, divided into parties according to their respective religions, turn the spit, *i.e.* they make a paste of millet, water, and fat, and then bake this so-called chipatti in the form of an omelette over the open fire. And this chipatti is the invariable menu of these poor creatures from year's end to year's end. If they can ever succeed in procuring such additions as vegetables, fruit, berries, herbs, fish, or meat, they are simply rolled up in the paste. But how few of them ever have anything to roll!

They all talk a lot at the top of their voices, whilst the food is conveyed by their fingers into their wide-open mouths to the accompaniment of much lively gesticulation. They seem to be trying to out-scream one another, and an onlooker would certainly think they were quarrelling violently. As a matter of fact, they never get excited, and the subject of their conversation is utterly unimportant. The poor devils are only rejoicing that the heat and burden of the day are past, and that they can at last enjoy their rest and chipatti—whether rolled or empty,—more especially as this evening meal is their chief meal of the day.

An Indian day is only twice enlivened by the joys of the table; but the meagre refreshment taken in the middle of the day is made up for by uncomfortably large portions in the evening. I am continually astonished at the amount of millet-cake and fresh water which are consumed in our camp on all sides with ease and comfort.

Gradually the noise becomes hushed, the fires die down, and Night makes good her claims.

Long after the privileged are sleeping peacefully

under sheltering canvas, the poor bearers are trying to cuddle up nearer and nearer to the smouldering wood, wrapping their chipatti-filled bodies in their everyday clothing, with no addition for the night. In their squatting position the white burnous covers them from head to ankle, leaving the feet uncovered—impervious to any amount of cold.

Deep stillness descends upon our camp. From the distance comes a festive rustle, and close by is a murmuring and splashing—the secret colloquies of myriads of rills all wandering on their way to the sea. What an enchanting, thrilling melody!

I remain where I am, sunk deep in dreams and thought.

The stars twinkle above me. The Milky Way spreads its shining path—an unending chain of worlds running on into eternity. Devoutly and fervently do I dive deep into the silvery light of the heavens, trying there to cool and solve many a burning question or doubt.

CHAPTER XXI

A STRUGGLE WITH GRASS-SHOES

THREE o'clock in the morning. A burning candle lights up my tent. Varadara tears me from the arms of Morpheus. It is icy cold. One scarcely dares to dip one's finger-tips into the water.

"Sultana begs permission to enter and put on Sahib's grass-shoes."

And whilst I am eagerly swallowing my warm tea, he tries to force my feet into these unaccustomed fetters.

"Impossible; I shan't be able to walk twenty steps in these things."

"All Sahibs wear them," says Paul reassuringly.

Just imagine: thick woollen stockings more like our mittens, with felt slippers the same shape over them, and on the top of that sandals and plaited straw.

With natural Indian skill and quickness, Sultana pulls my toes apart for the third time in the attempt to get a rope as thick as my finger between them. Having at last succeeded, he twists it several times round my ankle with the remark, "Now they'll keep!"

I make gallant attempts to walk. "My big toe, my ankles! And I am supposed to walk for miles and climb mountains tied up like this! Well, I'll try; but let the tiffin coolies take shoes and stockings with them in case of emergency." I hobble on somehow.

The moon is shining in all her glory. "Good old friend, do you sympathise with me? Oh, these awful fetters!"

"Be very careful," warn the shikaris, supporting me on each side.

And now we come to a steep decline. Sultana and Samdu use their sticks as brakes, and plant their feet with care and precision. The surface is as shiny as glass and quite devoid of trees and bushes—not a thing to catch hold of or to stop one from slipping. Ever steeper and more precipitous does the path become. We slide and slip, and our sticks are bent nearly double. I sway. But it is wonderful how tightly my feet stick to the ground; they seem to be positively glued on, and they hold my body upright and help me to recover my balance.

Most slippery of all are the grass-grown precipices. Long grass, pressed down by the winter snow, now thawed, covers the underlying ground as if rolled in by a steam-roller. Even hobnailed boots would slip here—straw alone gives one a firm foothold.

Now begins the steep upward climb. The plaited straw takes a firm hold, and the toes, able to move freely in the sandals, give what help they can. Good old shoes, you did not deserve to be sworn at! And how comfortable they are now after a little bit of rope-dancing practice! Not a bit of pinching any more! And yet so tightly bound, so light, and so flexible!

[To face page 66.

SULTANA AND SAMDU HAVE SUCCEEDED IN TYING ME UP IN GRASS-SHOES.

CHAPTER XXII

GOREL

WE must have been climbing for about an hour and a half, grass-grown precipices, stony ground, rocks, and a bushy undergrowth presenting difficulties turn and turn about. Now Sultana calls a halt, and each of the three shikaris takes a handful of earth and lets it trickle through his fingers.

"The wind is in our favour."

Slowly the face of the moon grows paler. Icy air makes me shiver, bathed as I am in sweat after the hard climb. Samdu, well acquainted with the locality, now creeps forward on all fours and takes a stealthy look round, studying the distance through the telescope. We follow him as noiselessly as possible, and I get ready to shoot under cover of some low-growing bushes. Gradually dawn approaches, and then outlines of the nearest objects can be more plainly recognised every moment.

A deathlike stillness reigns, broken only from time to time by the harsh cry of a vulture. I am trembling in every limb, shivering with cold. Day comes quickly.

We are lying on the top of a narrow ridge. Below us are piles of gigantic rocks, opposite to us bare, desolate mountains ; behind us a whole row of mountain-tops follow closely one on the other, and on the horizon glitter snowy summits of an unimaginable height.

So far we have not been able to sight any game through our glasses. An enormous vulture sweeps past us, quickly followed by a second, and with the aid of the telescope I can see about thirty of these giants on a projecting rock not far off. They have spent their night there, and now fly valleywards one after the other.

At this moment Samdu creeps close up to me.

"Bara gorel," he whispers, and points across the chasm.

I can see nothing.

"Bara, bara," he repeats eagerly.

But I can still see nothing.

Now Unkar, too, pretends to be able to see the gorel, and turns nimbly to me with raised finger.

"Ek," he nods. "One buck."

But utterly in vain are the efforts of both to make clear to me the spot where the beast is standing. They take aim with my rifle, make signs with their arms and hands. They begin to get impatient, gesticulate, and try to make themselves understood in words—their whispering becomes more and more emphatic, louder and louder.

All to no purpose! If they were to scream aloud, I still could not understand their language.

"In which direction is he? Is it far off?" I ask in English, forgetting that they speak nothing but Kashmiri.

By Jove! Suddenly I, too, catch sight of something moving. A yellowish-brown creature, so difficult to distinguish against the same-coloured background that it is almost invisible even through the telescope, and so far away that even with the aid of the latter it would be impossible to hit him.

The gorel is feeding far below us, slowly making his way up the mountain-side opposite. Now he climbs quicker, stands still, listens, looks round, goes on feeding.

We lie motionless. I try with the glass to form some idea of his head adornments.

"Bara," whisper the shikaris—but does not the Indian always express himself in superlatives?

Meanwhile the buck has turned round, and is now feeding in the opposite direction, going ever further and further away from us, until he at last disappears behind a rock.

"Nothing to be done at present!" Such is the unwelcome news which Unkar conveys to me by signs. We jump up to try to cut him off. If only we had a Zeppelin-ship now! Or if we could at least get across the chasm along the top of the ridge! But no, in order not to be seen, we must climb down the side of the slope. The shikaris take my rifle, telescope, and cartridges, and, keeping me between them in the steep places, land me safely on the other side in ten minutes. Soon afterwards we reach the projecting rock. I lie down, creep forward, and warily raise my head. Sure enough, there he stands before me, about four hundred yards off, staring straight at me! Can he have got wind of us, or did he hear the falling stones?

I quickly screw the telescope on to my rifle behind a sheltering bush, rest my arm on a rock, using Samdu's puggree as a cushion, take aim and shoot.

"Missed him!"

The buck makes off at a tremendous rate.

But what's that? Suddenly he stops dead, and the next moment down he rolls from rock to rock into the abyss below.

Two of the men go after him, and return a little later carrying his skin and head.

"Bara?" I call out to them.

"Bara, bara," comes back the cheerful answer.

The wonderful gorel turns out to be a chamois!

I could have got that with considerably less trouble in the Egern Mountains!

CHAPTER XXIII

COLONEL WARD'S BOOK ON CASHMERE GAME

ONCE more back in camp I find letters awaiting me —thanks to the friendly ministrations of the Tassildar of Uri.

"Bad weather," "A wet, cold summer," "We still have fires going," is part of the news from home, in letters dated May 5th.

There is also a letter from Joe Phelps from Srinagar, whence comes the complaint, "Terrible drought, unbearable heat." He sends me a pamphlet written by his predecessor, Colonel Ward, who for thirty years had hunted and shot in the Himalayas as chief overseer of the Government preserves in Cashmere. There is a good deal of instruction to be got out of that little book.

"Gorel: the chamois of Central Asia. It is to be found on all the heights at the beginning of the Himalayas. Very shy and quick, and quite at home on most difficult ground, this graceful animal affords excellent sport. Its horns are straight, and resemble in shape and size those of its European cousin."

The Colonel mentions no less than twenty-eight different kinds of horned and antlered game to be found amongst the Cashmere Mountains: stags, goats, ibex, chamois, sheep, and antelopes of all breeds. He describes the manifold varieties of head-attire existing amongst them—all sizes, all shapes. What a freak of Nature!

"In the width and thickness of its antlers and branches the barasingh of Cashmere is not far behind the wapiti. And where is the sportsman whose heart will not beat harder when stalking the markhor, at sight of this king of the rocks, with his majestic, spreading, twisting horns, peculiar to himself!"

I come across such names as: "Ibex, thar, seror, gorel, ovisammon, ovispolei, oorial, charpoo, narpoo, burheel, sambur, musk-deer, barking-deer, heran-antelope, guttarosa-antelope, etc. etc." Deer, stags, sheep, and goats of the most uncommon varieties which live in the Cashmere Mountains, and, in company with the yellow panther, the snow-panther, black and red bears, wolves and wild dogs attract legions of sportsmen to their wild home and spur them on to deeds of daring enterprise.

Cashmere! A country three times as big as Switzerland, and nearly three times as high! Here there is plenty of room for game of all sorts, and they can find a home in any storey they choose—in the region of everlasting snow, in the land of rock, in the bottomless chasms of the great heights, on the barren, outlying hills and in the fertile plains with highly cultivated slopes. No railway has as yet desecrated this animal Paradise.

Only a few paths unite the few solitary and far-apart human dwellings during the summer months. India's Switzerland is up to now a world unto itself, whose inhabitants depend chiefly upon the fertile valley of Srinagar—a long narrow basin, not much larger than the county of Kent. All around and above it tower the mountains, making ingress and egress impossible with their snow and ice during six months of the year, and even rendering the path of the trespasser far from easy in the height of summer.

To the wild animals alone do they offer protection and refuge. For them their icy nature melts even during the winter deep down on the southern precipices, so that their four-legged guests shall never feel the pangs of hunger.

CHAPTER XXIV

THE PUNCH PASS

THERE are still five sheep alive. Roast gorel—I had succeeded in shooting three more fairly good bucks—helped to obtain for them a short reprieve. But the poor quintet grows visibly thinner as it follows us day by day, pitifully bleating forth its woes.

"The red one is to be killed last of all. He is my very good friend. Don't forget this, you heartless old cook!"

Or does this reproach really apply to myself? For the poor sheep has got to go sooner or later. The greater the love, the greater the egoism. Poor things! How often do they stop and try to still their hunger by nibbling at the sparse grass and weedy plants on the way! No good! The coolies and the cook are always there to drive them mercilessly onward.

We continue our march southwards in the direction of the Punch Pass. The ascent is so gentle that one scarcely notices it, but deep snowdrifts, driven thither by the strong wind, surround the pass.

In vain does the eye here seek high summits, nothing but low hills lying all round, in the form of rocky cupolas and minarets. It is a God-forsaken spot, a mixture of a jungle of low brushwood and bare, desolate high-land covered with snow.

It is only with difficulty and very slowly that my bearers manage to cover the ground, for their athletic shoulders are heavily burdened. In spite of the cold, their shiny bodies are bathed in sweat. Except for a loin-cloth, they are completely naked. They chatter amongst themselves the whole time and toil and drudge to provide me with comforts later on: a tent to shelter me, a warm bed, food and drink. Poor devils! Even the snail is only compelled to carry her own house on her back. She is not forced to groan beneath another's burdens and then made to sleep in the open. But you, poor devils, have to sweat and freeze in other men's service for the sake of a paltry two annas!

And yet it is just these men who so mercilessly drive on the poor, hungry sheep and expect them at the same time to get fat for eating. The rich alone feel compassion—thanks to an uneasy conscience!

At last the bearers are obliged to make a halt and rest. The shikaris and I continue our march.

The air is icy in spite of the prickling rays from above. Not a living thing is to be seen. Only the fresh tracks of a snow-leopard cross our path.

What can he find to interest him in this desolate world?

"More than likely that he has already made up his mind that our mutton would make him a very good supper to-night," says Paul.

We follow his tracks, but without success, and meanwhile the chiprassi has arranged the camp.

We spend the night on this side of the pass, and a bitterly cold one it is too. I shiver in my sleep in spite of my puschtin—a Thibetan fur sleeping-rug.

Poor wretched bearers! lying out in the starlight in your thin burnous beside a tiny fire, for sticks are not easily to be found in this snow-desert. But what would have been the good of one single puschtin to you all, even if I had not only felt, but also acted according to the Bible?

CHAPTER XXV

THE PIR PUNJAL

WE get a magnificent view from the top of the pass. In the east lies the gigantic chain of the Himalayas, clothed in eternal snow, furrowed by glaciers. In front of us, towards the south, a broken line of uneven points shooting up into the sky proclaims the kingdom of Pir Punjal.

How bare and blunt and yet how tremendous does Nature show herself here! No cathedral was ever large enough for me. It is true that Gothic pillars have often astonished my eye, but all the magnificence of art never touched my soul. The red and green windows obscure our view, as do also the star-bespangled ceilings, created to protect the work of man from cold and damp.

What a contrast do the works of God present! No wandering here over tombstones in the form of a cross—rather do our feet tread on mighty rocks towering in boundless leaps towards the zenith, bathed in the unclouded glow of the world's light.

Here every stone lives, whereas in the cathedrals life is turned to stone.

Steep, rocky walls descend sheer into the dark chasms below us, only to appear again later as pale green streaks in the far distance.

Far away, down below there, Spring is laughing.

We hurry on. Climbing, slipping, stumbling or falling over a wild, stony desert, we come upon underwood, thick forests or sparsely wooded regions traversed by stony, gravel, sandy, mossy or leaf-mould paths leading into green meadows of a celestial beauty.

How quickly does Nature change her gown in the Himalayas! Winter and summer side by side, also poverty and luxury, death and life. Down here in the pass there is a perfect carnival of Alpine flora after the long winter sleep beneath snow and ice. In the ravines and valleys, on the banks of the rushing streams and streamlets are positive forests of reeds and bulrushes. Red, green, and white berries peep out from betwixt pale green leaves. Climbing roses wreathe garlands amongst the thick branches of these northern maples, birches, and willows. Chestnuts, walnut-trees, cedars, firs—ornamental giants armoured in bark—arch themselves into shade-giving canopies, so thick that daylight can scarcely force its way through. A thousand mighty pillars uphold these arches, their capitals merging into the green roof.

All around the sweet-scented wood gives forth its treasures.

On the treeless edges of the valley the starry edelweiss shines pure and white, whilst at her feet, on a soft green carpet, violets, forget-me-nots, irises, primulas, and tulips spread their many-hued rays—myriads of rubies, sapphires, and pearls! A glistening girdle of gardens in the midst of a desolate highland wilderness, enlivened by the gentle humming of bees as they skim from flower to flower. Nature has it all her own way here—no need for her to make room for the greed of gold, which cuts the flowers, fells the trees, and ploughs the fields with an unloving, uncaring hand. Here, in the intoxication of Spring, Nature's children laugh and play and tease each another in the most charming of masquerades, each one dressed in his or her Sunday best.

The flowers make the most of this their one chance, for they have but these few short days to rejoice and bloom and shed their sweet scent around them. June and July are the only two months free from frost and snow. What a wrestle of Nature's eternal youth with the rotting, destroying strength of reality from which none of us are spared!

No human being lives here. All the louder do the waters splash and the birds sing; all the more do the butterflies skim about, the squirrels bustle, the bees hum, and the gnats tease in the witchery of the life-giving sunshine. Laughingly mischievous nymphs make love to each other, and modest naiads mirror the pretty femininity of their slender limbs in crystal-clear, silvery pools. What silence, void of man, which tells more than any amount of speech !

With intense pleasure I take long breaths of this bracing mountain air and bathe myself with delight in the sweet scents of this Alpine Paradise.

CHAPTER XXVI

SPRING IN THE VALLEY

WHEREVER berries and fruit are to be found, Black Bruin is sure not to be far off. His limbs are still somewhat heavy and stiff from their long winter sleep, but his greedy tummy is already beginning to rumble. He would willingly lay down his life for fruit, chestnuts, and fresh herbs. Completely ignoring the human intruder, Master Bruin sticks tight to the trees and bushes, filling his eager mouth with all the delicacies he can find. So, at least, many an Indian sportsman has told me ; and it is therefore not particularly difficult, especially in autumn, to secure these black rascals by the dozen.

But it is quite a different matter with his red cousin. In high-lying, desolate, rocky districts the latter spends his solitary, modest existence, living on plants, roots, dead game, squirrels, mice, snakes, and other vermin. His rough, lonely life amongst the heights has made him timid and nervous, and in his over-cautiousness his sense of smell and hearing have to serve him well. Long before one can even catch sight of him, he has taken to his heels and shuffled off.

Like all greedy creatures, our black friend of the valley is much thicker skinned. Like them, too, he is spiteful and quarrelsome. Directly he is wounded, his temper becomes awful, and, bursting with rage, the black bear will attack anything or anybody that he thinks may have been the cause of his pain. He will often revenge himself on one of his own tribe if he cannot at once get at the actual ill-doer. Failing any other, his best friend may come in for a sounding box on the ears, and if there are several of them anywhere near, a bloody hand-to-hand fight is likely to ensue. The sportsman who happens to be a spectator at one of these impromptu battles may, with luck, get in several good shots and go off laden with spoil.

It is best to stalk the bear when he is either on the same level or lower down than oneself, because the best and strongest animal can only climb upwards in a very clumsy fashion, and one has therefore plenty of time to take sure aim. Downhill, on the other hand, the angry black bear can rush with tremendous and quite unexpected speed, no matter how rough and stony his path may be. Woe betide his assailant if he miss his mark !

CHAPTER XXVII

AFTER A BLACK BEAR

For two long, hot days, from morning to night, through thick and thin, I had been on my legs; but all to no purpose! Master Bruin was nowhere to be seen.

"A month later," said the shikaris. "The fruit and the berries are not yet ripe enough. His lordship likes them very sweet."

There are crowds of hares and partridges; but as soon as the shooting season opens, a thousand reasons are forthcoming by way of excuse for the unexpectedly poor bags. Are not men and women, including sportsmen, just the same all the world over?

In order to get a better bird's-eye view, we climbed up to the top of the ridge, and thence scoured the hillside with our glasses, going carefully over every turn, spying into every corner, staring hard at every fruit tree, and even inspecting the hollow trunks of chestnuts and deodar cedars. All in vain! Not a bear to be seen! Nothing but crowds of monkeys, that with their children and grandchildren accompany us like so many rope-dancers from bough to bough and from tree to tree, only to turn back suddenly and hide themselves in the thick foliage.

At last the shikaris come across some fresh bear tracks, with some overturned stones near them—a promising sign. Samdu and Sultana regard each overturned pebble with solemn attention, and at last come to the conclusion that the tracks are those of a bara balu, a male bara balu.

"It is white ants that they hunt for under the stones," and the shikaris poke out a few of these insects with their sticks.

"They are the same beastly creatures as those that flew into the Count Sahib's soup last night, only that these have not yet got any wings."

I heartily praise the bear's industry, and wish that he would eat them all up, skin and bones and wings, these nasty, unappetising, pestilent insects!

"But what a lot of stones poor old Bruin would have to turn over to fulfil this inhuman wish of mine! And how often would he draw a blank!"

"No, Sahib; the bear can scent them out from beneath the biggest rocks, and he never turns over a stone in vain."

Several times we thought we had sighted the ant-hunter; but each time it was only a wild boar. And precious little notice they took of us!

"There's another of those bristly beasts!"

"No! Balu!"

"Do!"

"Sure enough! Two bears!"

Slowly they were winding their way amongst some brushwood on the dark side of the hill. I wanted to try and get a shot at them with the help of the telescope, but the target became more indistinct every minute, and at last the two animals disappeared beneath the bushes. We caught one or two more glimpses of their silhouettes, but always at a greater distance off, and before long the veil of evening hid them from our sight.

CHAPTER XXVIII

FORTY WINKS

The next morning we hurry back to the same spot, but of course no bear to be seen as far as the eye can reach or our legs can carry us. At last the midday heat forces us to give up the search.

I empty out the contents of my thermos apparatus : chicken with rice ! How delicious this might be ! But this pappy mixture ! Rice and "rice," chicken and "chicken," the soul of man and the "soul of man" separated from each other by a world-wide gulf !

"Ram Sheik, you big-mouthed boaster, soulless, narrow-minded cook ! You can only boil—boil things to bits !"

CHAPTER XXIX

A GOOD BAG

A TUG at my arm awakens me out of a sweet sleep.

"Balu," whispers Sultana.

Not more than a hundred and fifty yards above our resting-place a bear is slouching slowly along. In a second I have seized my loaded rifle, and take aim in a kneeling position.

"He will stand still in a minute, Sahib."

I go with him. But as a target he becomes less and less clear, and eventually disappears behind a tree. I put down my gun and look at the shikaris for instructions. They make excited signs.

Sure enough, the bear is again visible; there he stands in all his majesty beneath a tree, hunting for berries. Crack!

"A good shot, I think. Have I hit him? Or has he got off?"

"We had better wait a bit," says Sultana. Then he arms himself with both my rifles, whilst Samdu and Unkar draw their hunting-knives. Cautiously we make towards the spot at which I aimed, I in the middle.

"We've got him," calls Sultana.

What a pity! His skin is useless. The sun has already deprived him of his winter coat.

CHAPTER XXX

A MOUNTAIN PARADISE

AND now we must leave this Alpine oasis. Farewell, ye flowers!

The trees keep us company for quite a long time—they all seem anxious to come with us, from the tenderest sapling to the thousand-year-old patriarchs.

They are still unacquainted with man and his little ways—they do not yet look upon him as Fate—a cruel Fate that pulls them up by the roots or fells them at a stroke. So far they have only had to wrestle with time, snow, and gales. Many a one lies on the ground covered with leaves and trailing plants. New generations rise up in their place, and everywhere they stand, side by side, in various degrees either of development or decay: childhood, youth, prime, infirmity, old age. But the Song of Eternity resounds through all their branches, and with silent salutations old and young take leave of us.

The scenery now begins to change with kaleidoscopic rapidity—winding valleys, waterfalls leaping down steep hillsides, difficult passes, and fertile meadows confront us in succession.

But no sign of game anywhere. This is the more extraordinary as it seems a perfect Eldorado for wild creatures, with its splendid grazing ground, running water, and complete lack of disturbing elements.

It is, of course, no use setting our hopes on barasingh in these heights ; but all the different kinds of mountain sheep, goats, and ibex, where can they be ?

They are faithful to the snow and make their dwelling wherever their white friend decrees. Only the last degree of necessity can induce them to leave it and come down lower. Their hunger satisfied, they return as quick as may be to their old home, climbing with sure foot over rough and stony paths. Here only do they feel themselves in their element, beyond the reach of human machinations, under cover of rocky chasms, hidden from sight and protected from the burning rays of the noonday sun. And just below the snow-line, on the steepest hillsides, in the crevices of the most slippery rocks, and in the clefts of the most perpendicular precipices grow the sweetest and best-tasting grasses and herbs, watered by virginal drops of melted snow, and far more luscious than any that the sun himself can bring to life.

One never finds many different kinds of animals living close together. They keep themselves to themselves with tribal pride, seeking their food on quite different mountains at various heights. Here chamois, there antelopes or wild sheep ; here again goats, there stags or ibex. And, besides this, each flock or herd has its own distinct region to which it strictly adheres.

CHAPTER XXXI

LALI, THE RED SHEEP

"DURING the next two days the Sahib won't get a chance of coming upon any big game." Thus the shikaris.

I therefore take my gun and shoot a few chicoris. I hope no one will tell tales to the Game Department at Srinagar, for these birds are supposed to be having their close time now!

But Major Wigram is far away, and I shoot. Somewhat larger than our partridge, and with reddish feathers, these shy birds of the valley afford a delicious dish of roast game. In contradistinction to their behaviour in the valley, they are almost tame up here on the hills, and are as little shy as the wild-boars, three of which I soon shot—for the sake of my men.

Two would really have been enough for them, had not the two first died before the Mohammedans, rushing up, could cut their throats. Under these conditions alone will the pious Moslem consent to eat them. At sight of Sultana's and Samdu's sulky faces,

I therefore shot a third one, this time in his seat of honour, leaving the rest to the Koran. Be not disgusted, you Europeans, accustomed to observe the etiquette of sport! It means a wild chase after the wounded game, followed by a desperate sawing with blunt knives at the throat of the wretched animal whilst in its death-agony. What a horribly cruel proceeding—and all in honour of Mahomet! At last they have made a great gash, the blood rushes out, praise be to Allah! And now the shikaris, with a conscience at rest, and mouths watering, once more take the lead.

The sides of the mountain begin to get more rocky, but are still well covered with grass; our path continues upwards over treeless spaces, interspersed by green wavy lines—the verdant banks of the many streams hurrying and tumbling downhill towards us. One might easily imagine oneself in Thuringia, to judge by the complete absence of mountains—they seem to have disappeared into space.

These are gala days for my poor sheep. There are still five of them to enjoy the fresh green pasture. The cook has not yet sharpened his knife!

I must beg forgiveness for again speaking of these four-legged creatures. But, later on, up in the snow, there is not a butcher's or poulterer's shop to be found at every corner. Up there they must play an important part as cold buffet.

My red friend has become quite friendly; he

PAUL EXAMINES LALI. IS HE FAT ENOUGH TO KILL?

comes when I call him, and nibbles bread out of my hand, and then tries to buck at me. Not much to choose between animals and men, except that the former repulse one in ignorance after receiving favours!

I call the red sheep "Lal," and later on "Lali." This strikes the shikaris and coolies as queer behaviour on my part, and they are beginning to see something more than skin and bones in this poor sheep.

CHAPTER XXXII

A RUSSIAN PRINCE

THREE messengers, sent by the Tassildar, catch us up. They bring rice, millet, flour, potatoes, and several bits of news.

"There is another white Sahib following behind us. He can't be far off now. They say he is a Russian Prince and that he has engaged a crowd of bearers and pays enormously high wages. He is also going to shoot markhor in the Numlah Nullah!"

Bazaar gossip, of course! The Indian is always eager to hear and to tell something new.

Paul draws a long face, and the shikaris want to press forward to the markhor gorge before the Russian Prince can get there.

"Ridiculous nonsense! The times are long past when white men ran races for the best game regions. All shooting matters are now severely settled by rule-of-three at the Srinagar Game Department. Each aspirant receives a clearly defined district, and may only shoot a certain number of heads of game. For every sixty rupees one is entitled to shoot two markhors, two ibex, two barasinghs, two black bears, and one red bear. I was told to go in this direction, and the Numlah Nullah was parcelled off to me for markhor. I shall, therefore, be the only man shooting there this spring. The Russian may have been given a neighbouring district."

"And perhaps, after all, it is only a British subaltern," says Paul. "Numbers of them are scattered over the Cashmere Mountains, shooting and fishing, every spring and autumn."

"Tell the bearers not to get so excited; let them hear the magic word backshish," I say to Sultana; "but don't forget to add the important 'if,'—if the Sahib gets a good markhor."

It is very rare to come across foreigners in these mountains. Englishmen, on the other hand, wander over them in crowds every year. There is scarcely a single young officer or official who does not make an expedition to the Himalayas as soon as he can after getting to India. Each one of them hopes to make a record, and to accomplish this they are even willing to stand their polo-sticks and cricket-bats in the corner for three months of the year. They strap their belt tighter, train heart and muscles till they are as hard as iron, and start, filled with the one desire to bring back the best head or to shoot the rarest animal at the greatest height. They are no wholesale murderers, these English Nimrods. They do their stalking with a yard-measure in their pockets.

They only lie in wait for the longest antlers—every extra inch forming an addition to their triumph.

Thus every spring and autumn a regular competition takes place in the Cashmere mountain-world, and not only there, but also at the capital, Srinagar, and all over the valley, thoughts are given up to big-game shooting and records.

CHAPTER XXXIII

THAR

THE 13th June 1909 seemed to be going to be a lucky day. At dawn, already, the shikaris reported having seen a herd of thar, with several good bucks amongst them. And we even succeeded in getting within shooting distance of them. But oh, that trickiness of fate, about which Professor Fischer has written quite a big book!

"A slice of bread-and-butter always falls on the buttered side!"

This time it was stones that fell. A miniature land-slip suddenly started helter-skelter on its journey just above the spot where the herd was quietly grazing. Loosened by the spring sunshine, the pebbles tumbled head over heels into the valley and frightened the thar away.

They look very much like our domestic ram, but their horns are a good deal shorter.

In the course of the same day I had the luck to get a shot at three bears and one musk-deer.

Out of them all I only succeeded in hitting one black bear.

And I was particularly keen, too, on getting the musk-deer, with its two long tusks hanging down. Paul was as disappointed as I was, and went about all day with a miserable face. The animal's glands would have been worth, at least, thirty rupees to the poor fellow, and he could have lived in comfort on that for three months, or have passed, at least, one pleasant evening in the company of a bazaar beauty.

The musk-deer is generally very timid and difficult to approach, but this particular one was unusually tame, and the bears, too, made excellent targets of themselves. Nevertheless, I missed them all except the one old Bruin. What else can you expect on the 13th?

"Strange to find black bears so high up," remarked the shikaris; for we were getting into pretty high regions by now, where meadows and pasture-land disappear, and nothing but thin grass vegetating amidst rocks and stones takes their place. Fewer and fewer become the fir-trees that stand out sharply against the grey and yellow background. Slowly they are awaking from their long winter sleep, blinking their budding eyes and stretching their slender limbs towards the northern Spring: here and there delicate little branches show the birth of a new life.

For the first time since we began our ascent, the sun sometimes deserts us during the afternoon. Grey clouds, driven quickly along by the wind, envelop the mountains and us in their cold embrace. Thus do earth and sky disclose to each other their secrets.

CHAPTER XXXIV

CAPTURING A RED BEAR

The higher we get the more imposing do the mountains become; wild, dark chasms, sharp, rugged cliffs, and bare, weather-beaten precipices surround us on all sides.

Old Father Time has produced these wonders, and Mother Nature has brought all her powers to bear upon these mountains. Sun and frost, heat and cold, air and water, ice and snow, every plant, from the finest blade of grass to the sturdiest oak, every creature, from the smallest worm to man himself, gnaws at their vitals.

Water is the mountains' worst enemy. Every drop helps to hollow out the stone; rivulets and streamlets chisel out channels for themselves and fill up every hole and crevice, so that later on, when frozen hard, not even the largest rocks can withstand their pressure. Nature is never idle—quarries are made picturesque, and life and beauty instilled into all objects that her finger touches. A few isolated, tall trees triumph above the rocks. They had to suffer much in their childhood and youth, but now they are all the more sure of their ground, and their power of resistance is all the greater for the hardships endured.

Wrapped in mist, and very indistinct, white cliffs rise up in the far distance. In the clefts and crevices the last decaying winter snow is dragging out a miserable existence, dropping big, dirty tears over its sad fate. Cheerful little streams trickle gently over the stones, and miniature avalanches slide mischievously down into the valleys below. Head over heels they go, their silvery bodies mirrored in a thousand glistening reflections; for the sky, yesterday so deeply veiled, has once more opened its big blue eyes.

About five o'clock in the afternoon we catch sight of a dark object at some distance off. It seems to be moving.

"Upon my word, if it isn't a bear!"

"We shall have to be awfully careful how we approach the old chap, for it can only be a red bear at this height."

We let a little powdery snow trickle through our fingers to get the direction of the wind. The bear is digging hard in the snow, quite unsuspecting.

"I expect he is digging out the carcase of an ibex that died in the winter, and that'll keep him busy for several hours. It's just possible that we shall be able to get within shooting distance of him."

We begin our flank attack by marching through several narrow defiles, keeping an eye on Bruin, who is still hard at work on his cold repast. It gives him a lot of trouble, but how he will enjoy it in the end!

We are, however, still much too far off to risk a shot. Eight hundred yards, at least, still lie between us and our prey. We dare not go straight on, as there is no cover whatever, and impassable ravines make a roundabout way out of the question.

So there is nothing to be done but to wait and watch; and this we do for about one and a half hours.

Naughty old Bruin gives us a hard lesson in patience; but at last he seems to have eaten his fill. He stops digging, stands still buried in thought, raises his head, walks round his field of action, stands still again, looks all round, and stares motionless in our direction for several minutes. Then he begins to waddle off towards us, goes slower, sniffs, eyes our hiding-place, turns over a few stones and sticks his snout into everything. Suddenly he disappears into the hollow just below us.

"Two hundred and fifty yards," whispers Sultana. "If only he would come up again now!"

I think it is more than 250 yards. The natives have, it is true, splendid eyesight, but they are not good judges of distance.

It must be at least a good 400 yards. That means aiming higher, for my telescope stands at 175 yards.

Scarcely daring to breathe, I lie still, holding my rifle. Sultana puts his puggree on the rock, so that I can rest my arm on it in case of necessity.

I aim once or twice, and notice that the light is excellent. If only he would come!

But no bear appears! What a bitter disappointment!

"The wind is against us. He is certain to have gone back through the defile."

"Stay! What's that?" And at the same moment Sultana gives my sleeve a tiny tug. I seize my rifle.

"Is it a wild boar?"

No! A large red bear not 100 yards in front of me! He's off in big bounds! I am on the point of pulling the trigger when he suddenly stops at the edge of the ravine, turns round towards me, and sniffs suspiciously. Now!

"He's hit! I heard the bullet strike him."

But the bear disappears over the edge, out of sight.

Sultana and I follow him quickly. No signs of blood to be seen where he stood. Very cautiously we peep into every possible hiding-place. We separate, Sultana going over to the opposite bank. Carefully, from bush to bush and from rock to rock, we continue our search. I see the shikari stop with a jerk. He looks through the glasses, raises his rifle, takes aim and shoots, shoots again, and then bursts into a loud shout of joy.

Samdu and Unkar hurry up. I follow.

"Lal balu!"

"Lal, lal!"

And a large red bear rolls down towards me.

"How did it happen? What did he do? Where was he? Was he going to attack you? Why did you shoot twice?"

"Lal balu, Sahib, lal, lal!"

A red bear! What an unusual bit of luck!

I can only find one bullet in his beautiful thick coat—in at the neck, out at the shoulder.

These modern rifles are very exact, even at long distances, but they do not cause the game to fall at once when hit. And that is just what one wants in India's and Africa's thick jungles, which make the search so difficult, and where one may need protection against the sudden charge of big game.

"Where in the world can your bullets be, Sultana?"

He hangs his head in embarrassment and raises his hands apologetically. "The bear was already dead, Sahib; but I thought it best to be on the safe side——"

"When in doubt shoot twice, especially if you miss both times, old chief!" and, smiling, I shake hands with the good fellow.

"This time it is really a bara, bara—barissimo!"

MY FIRST RED BEAR.

CHAPTER XXXV

COLONEL WARD ON THE MARKHOR

Colonel Ward, in his little book, gives some statistics concerning the game shot in Cashmere during the last ten years. The average for red bears was 85 a year, and according to official information the largest was 7 feet 6 inches, measured from the eyes to the tail. No matter how I pull and drag at it, I can't get my skin to stretch to more than 6 feet 10 inches.

But I must be satisfied with what I have got, and I am indeed very pleased at getting a red bear at all. It is far easier to procure a black one, as the statistics show, 322 being the yearly average. It is almost the same proportion in numbers as that between the Cashmere cousins, markhor and ibex: 118 markhors as against 286 ibex.

The horns of the ibex are perhaps more handsome, making as they do such a charming arched line in profile; but every sportsman in Asia puts a higher value on the majestic, snake-like, twisted, slender antlers of the markhor. Then, too, ibex, though of inferior quality, can be got in other parts of the yellow continent, in Africa, and even in the Italian Alps; whereas the snowy heights of the Himalayas alone produce the markhor.

Some 20,000 rupees, in round numbers about £1,250, are added to the State coffers of Cashmere through the sale of shooting licences at 60 rupees apiece. About two hundred Europeans are responsible for this sum, and thereby add considerably to the otherwise rather scarce means of increasing the revenues of the country.

In this way, too, about three thousand coolies earn food and wages for six months of the year, and a few pence to carry them through the rest of the time. The natural products of the land bring in more, and especially Srinagar's merchants succeed in grabbing at many an exceptional price.

Lucky Dives! Poor Lazarus!

Part III

IN THE REALMS OF THE MARKHOR

CHAPTER XXXVI

THE NUMLAH NULLAH

We had reached the outlying ranges of the Numlah Nullah, and, so far, neither Russian nor Englishman had crossed our path. Those few men whom we encountered were of a duskier hue. Only the mountains became ever whiter and whiter — everything, rocks, cliffs, the snow itself, still unbesmirched by human foot, white—all white! The summit of Pir Panjal, with its silvery, jagged edges and crown of rocks, beckoned to us from a lofty height—a magnificent sight.

Not a breath of air, not a cloud in the sky, not a sign of mist! The snow-giant, though hundreds of miles away, seems to be quite close, so clearly is every peak, every curve outlined against the sky.

In a circular valley, bathed in sunshine, we set up our tents.

Here the greater part of the snow has already been conquered by its fiery enemy; young grasses and edelweiss nod their heads; venerable deodar-firs stand sentry before my tent. Straight and silent, these weather-beaten trees glisten with sundrops and wait patiently for Spring.

Rugged rocks, still more dignified, still more motionless, keep them company, guarding the secret of their own lives within invisible, fast-closed inner chambers. But even they develop, breathe, grow. The eternal law of progress has brought them into existence, helped them to increase up here amongst the highest points of the Himalayas. What a marvellous process of Nature !

Millions of snow-pearls drop in rhythmical regularity from the rocky cliffs. They have a long way before them to reach the ocean ; and many a yarn will they spin on their return. They will tell how they licked the stones, played with the pebbles, fought with the rocks, tore up trees by their roots, watered meadows, gave refreshment to man and beast, turned mill-wheels, washed away villages, bore mighty vessels on their bosoms, devoured them in their wrath, veiled the face of the sun, brought fertility and blessing, misery and destruction, and as white snow-flakes allowed children to play with them, buried human beings, covered whole mountains and suffocated Nature wholesale !

I wonder how they will treat me when I reach their icy realms ?

My men have no time for such dreamy reflections ; they think only of to-day, and with their stomachs. Shikaris and coolies are all busy collecting dead branches, digging out holes for the fires, filling the kettles with snow, and kneading dough for chipattis. Chipattis for ever! Never mind! They will sleep all the better later on—a sleep void of care. Do they ever dream, I wonder, or only of chipattis?

CHAPTER XXXVII

IN THE SNOW-BOUND REALMS OF THE MARKHOR

THE next morning, before starting, I take a good look round with the glasses.

"Beyond those high-wooded ridges, in ravines looking like burnt-out glaciers, lives the markhor," explains Sultana.

It means another six hours' march to get there. We were obliged to make our last halt here for fear of disturbing the game, as the outlying hills act as a screen between them and our noisy camp and tell-tale fires.

From time to time a dull rumbling sound, like a distant peal of thunder, reaches my ear, and black smoke-like clouds appear above the hill-summits.

"Landslips," is the laconic explanation offered by the stalkers.

"Those clouds in the distance are all dust. The noonday sun is thawing the ground, and rocks, stones and snow are melting and slipping," adds one, a little more talkative than the others.

I had often heard of the many dangers connected

with ibex-shooting—of the extreme slipperiness of the ground, of the steep precipices, the hidden chasms, and the sudden and unexpected avalanches. Going after game and plain mountaineering are two very different matters as regards danger. The mountaineer is not obliged to follow a given direction; he can choose the best route and can wait and consider. The man bent on shooting cannot weigh issues—he must do and dare, the game being his one cause for consideration.

And just the ibex and the markhor are to be found amongst the most difficult parts of the mountains.

Without assistance of any kind one has to approach them unseen, unheard, and with the wind in the right direction. The stalking cannot be accomplished over ground affording sure foothold; it must be done silently and quickly up and down steep places. No time to scoop out steps! On we go, climbing, slipping, clutching! The true sportsman does not care; his enthusiasm renders him blind and indifferent to danger, especially if he happens to be after wounded game. Too late when the avalanche comes, the slipping ground rumbles! Too late when one's foothold is lost never to be regained! The plant of destruction blossoms freely and quickly up here in these otherwise barren regions!

Again and again I hear the distant noise of thunder, and one after another thick clouds of dust hide the blue sky from my sight.

8

Will the markhor prove fatal to me? Surely not! It is only heroes who die! Ordinary mortals are in no danger! And I have never been warned by the white nuns, who know that I have as yet scattered no triglavroses, plucked no blue irises in the Happy Valley! Often and often have I longed to do so, for they are so lovely and they smell so sweet; but they are said to bring bad luck, so I resisted and turned away with a sigh. They are used in Cashmere for decorating graves—hence the legend of misfortune.

Poor, pretty blue flowers! What a sad lot is yours!

CHAPTER XXXVIII

AVALANCHES AND LAND-SLIPS

A FEW scattered firs still strive to keep us company; but now they are being left further and further behind in the snow. It is marvellous to what great heights these sturdy knights of the forest work their way up.

But stay! I am wrong!

It is rather the snow which goes down to meet them, for we are now scarcely 12,000 feet above the sea-level, and yet, in spite of the Indian June sun, the southern sides of the Himalayas still obstinately refuse to doff their white winter furs.

How much earlier do the giants of Central Asia and Thibet yield to the sun's rays! Even as early as May they are said to be entirely free of snow at a height of 15,000 feet above the level of the sea.

Paradoxical as it sounds, it is just the burning Indian sun which nourishes the Cashmere snow. It caresses it winter and summer, causing continual showers in the lower regions. Here its hot rays make the earth sweat and then suck up the moisture thus produced, in order to send it forth again on its perpetual journey as snow and rain.

Just the opposite takes place on the northern side of the Himalayas, where, owing to the lack of dew and mist, the ground never gets moistened during the hot season. It is scorched and burnt up whilst the sun shines, and only cools in time to freeze beneath winter's snow and ice.

This is the explanation of the extraordinarily high and low temperatures in these parts and of the comparatively mild winters and bearable summers on the Indian side. Water is always plentiful; refreshing storms take place all through the summer; and perpetual showers fertilise the plants and the soil.

The regular succession of sun and moisture promote the growth of a vegetation peculiar to the temperate zone, such as is nowhere in the world to be found in greater perfection. Our northern trees, flowers, and grains came originally from Cashmere, where they flourish luxuriously. In return we sent them potatoes and—roses!

In undreamed-of profusion the latter spread their sweetness all over the Happy Valley, running a close race with the homely potato. In every garden in Srinagar, on all the squares, all over the lawns, on the banks of the canals and rivers, up the houses and walls, and on the roofs and towers they carry on their mischievous games, winding themselves round everything, delighting with their gentle tricks, winning hearts and charming eyes with their colour and scent. You lovely roses! You beloved thorns!

But wherefore these sighs of longing? Am I not much nearer heaven up here, in these celestial heights as grand as the sea, as sublime as love, and just as variable and full of moods as either!

Cr—r—r—r—r——
Cra—cra—a—a——
Cra—cra—c—k—cr—a—a—ck.

Who does not recognise this language of our northern ice? And thus do these mountains, too, suddenly drag me back from the land of dreams.

I forget the roses and the thorns as well, and once more the glistening snow-spires in the distance act on me like a magnet. Onwards, into the icy morning! Icy, because the sun has not yet risen.

I have left the coolies, the tents, the wretched cook, and even faithful Paul, behind. Such is the will of the ibex! Three shikaris, four bearers with thick furs and blankets, baskets filled with mutton and chicken, and hot thermos bottles are all that are allowed me now. Each day coolies will supply us with fresh provisions.

Thank Heaven! the sun is rising higher and higher. With his advent winter departs and spring appears; the snow binds and the ice bursts. But I don't believe that summer will ever come to these lonely heights!

CHAPTER XXXIX

A FREEZING NIGHT

DENSE, woolly clouds sail away beneath us, leaving a pale sea of silver out of which peep forth glistening mountain crests in many fantastical shapes : ramparts and towers, battlements and ridges—every form one can imagine presented in the sharpest contrasts and most wonderful colour effects. Nowhere, probably, do light and shade produce greater marvels than here, where the sky is so clear and so near.

What a magic air-city—a new world ! And yet how lonely and lifeless ! Like a cold woman, lovely to look at, the rocks stand, passive and indifferent in their majestic beauty. No warmth of love, no neighbourly interest, no ambitious struggle —nothing but unchanging coldness, stony indifference, deathlike silence !

We have now reached the edge of Crass Nullah. About three hundred feet from its summit we call a halt, and prepare a stony camp beneath the shelter of a large, projecting rock. Thus we intend to camp every night—until I get him !

MY LAST HALT BEFORE ENTERING THE REALMS OF THE MARKHOR.

The burning day is followed by a bitter night, arctic cold on top of tropical heat. I cover myself up to my nose, and creep deeper and deeper into my puschtin, getting as close as I can to the shikaris and coolies—brown hearts can warm as well as white ones!

CHAPTER XL

THE MARKHOR SIGHTED AT LAST

MY morning tea is cold, and my poor inside is colder still after a freezing sleep on a mattress of granite.

Day is just dawning as we climb the last steps, and, holding our breath, take an eager peep into the realm of the markhor.

What shall we see behind that stony curtain? What do they look like, these Himalayan Zlatarogs? How will they show themselves? Will their mountain stronghold look different from the other mountains?

It is still too dark to answer any of these questions—so dark that we cannot even distinguish objects quite close to us. I wriggle forward on my stomach—without a sound, except for the loud beating of my heart—as far as the nearest projecting rock. Then I cautiously raise my head, stare down into the depths, squint towards each side, peep, listen, and try with every sense and muscle to penetrate the dark veil of dawn.

Gradually the shades of night give way, and minute by minute the nearest outlines become clearer. Armed with the useful Goerz glass, the eye is soon able to distinguish things on the furthest slopes, and by degrees even the most distant clefts and crevices, chasms and ravines, creeks and corners are exposed to our view.

But it is a world without life—nothing but stone and snow—a desolate wilderness of snowy mountain-tops, a labyrinth of abysses and passes, a chaos of perpendicular slopes and giddy precipices. Rock upon rock rises out of the depths, till the highest one seems to bear the heavens on its shoulders. Poetry in the raw, untouched by art, Nature's grand and desolate poetry! So melancholy in its lonely grandeur!

Not a single bird here chirps forth its morning song of praise. Not a murmur of running water is ever heard here. Even the avalanches are frozen and still at this early morning hour.

If there is no love up here, neither is there any other disease. Sin is also absent, for one cannot sin alone. A stillness as of the grave—death has strangled joy and laughter.

Almost colourless, the sun rises above the sea of rocks, regards us coldly, and mirrors himself with metallic sharpness in the snow and ice.

Sultana looks inquiringly at me, and, shrugging his shoulders, makes a negative gesture with his hands, "No Markhor." He gives me to understand by signs that I am to slide backwards.

Shivering with cold, I obey orders, and then, covered up behind a rock where there is no snow, try to move and stretch my frozen limbs.

Unkar and a bearer relieve me from the pressure of the sandals, rub my feet, and massage my legs, thus bringing new life into those benumbed extremities.

Sultana and Samdu, meanwhile, had gone off to reconnoitre further afield. Some hours later they return with beaming faces and cheerful news.

"We have seen five first-rate bucks. They were just settling down to rest. Will the Sahib follow us? But it is a long way, and dangerous."

CHAPTER XLI

COMING NEARER TO THE MARKHOR

SWIFTLY the shikaris bind on my grass shoes, pulling and dragging hard at the straw straps: they must sit specially tight to-day, for our path is sharp and slippery. Steep, rocky slopes, stony ramparts, and treacherous formations surround the kingdom of the markhor. And, warning me of all these dangers, my faithful men do their work well.

I fix my toupee tightly on my head, for the sun has now reached its zenith, and is sending down burning rays upon us.

My sportsman's heart beats high with hope.

But what mountains!

The shikaris climb like chamois, hanging on to the rocks with hands and feet, burdened as they are with my rifles. Unkar and Sultana hold my hands and steady themselves by their feet alone. They go like cats up the bare hillsides, and have to bear my weight into the bargain. No matter how I drag on them, they keep their balance, and climb lightly on. If I seem undecided, the good fellows pull me on, and if I try to resist they whisper, "Markhor! markhor!" This restores my courage, and I make fresh efforts. Shall we reach our destination safely? Our lives themselves end with a note of interrogation.

Good old sandals, where should I be without you now? Like the stalkers, you never leave me in the lurch, either on the slippery grass, amongst the rocks, or in the snow!

"Mercy! A moment's rest to get my breath!"

"It will be better directly, Sahib," says Sultana consolingly.

He is right. As if going up a winding staircase between the pillars of a Gothic fortress, we now climb up comparatively easily.

"They were lying down on the opposite side of that chasm. We have no time to lose, for they will begin to move at about five o'clock, and start off in search of food."

Only one more snowy valley to pass. It looks so harmless, too, just nice for sleighing!

"Count Sahib must wait a moment; we will scoop out some steps."

Sultana scratches out a hollow with the shovel-end of his stick big enough to take his heel, and quickly makes a second hole further on for the other foot, and so on step by step, slowly onwards. Samdu and Unkar follow in his footmarks, broadening and hardening each one in turn. The melted snow hardens almost immediately, and the extreme cold from the earth beneath soon causes the new steps to freeze afresh.

The ravine was about two hundred yards wide, and spread downwards in pleasant undulations for hundreds of yards.

Their work finished, the stalkers come back for me, and Sultana unwinds his puggree and tries to fasten me to himself.

"It is safer, Sahib. We are responsible for your safety."

"I will only take hold of your leash with one hand. I prefer to be on the safe side. You might slip yourself—then I should let go at once," is my unspoken and unchristianlike thought, as I twist Sultana's rose-coloured cloth—made in Germany—tightly round my wrist and prepare to follow him, whilst Samdu, Unkar, and the bearers bring up the rear. Thus, step by step, we cross the rocky arena.

It is a strange sensation. A single false step, a moment's giddiness, and down we go! Quite softly and slowly at first, then quicker and quicker—never to return!

One must not think of it.

"Markhor, markhor," pipe the shikaris. "We shall see them in a minute."

"They are still on the same spot," is Samdu's cheerful news a little later; for he had gone forward whilst I stopped to eat a mouthful of food.

Noiselessly we make our way over the last snow-covered barricades, creep to the very edge of the bulwarks, peep, *ventre-à-terre*, over the mass of bare rocks. But for a long time I can see nothing. In a toneless voice Samdu tries to direct my eager gaze. But still I cannot get a glimpse at the longed-for creatures.

At last! Now I think I see them, standing out like grey spots against the deep snow.

They are lying between some big boulders, and with the help of the telescope I can now see them quite distinctly.

With heads proudly raised, the markhor are staring down into the valley, their majestic horns standing out black against the white background. I can count five. The master-buck is lying in the front row, a little higher than the others.

"Quite impossible to get any nearer," gesticulate the stalkers. "The Sahib must wait until they go down to graze."

We squat on our haunches and watch them, never once removing our eyes or our glasses.

And there they lie, motionless as stone pagodas.

Still they do not move, though the sun is beginning to sink behind the mountains, and a wonderful sunset fills the valley with its fiery light.

At last the foremost buck gets slowly up. There he stands in the snow, a mighty creature with giant horns. He stretches his hairy body, raises his crowned head, lets his piercing glance sweep over his mountain kingdom. Here he is king by Divine Right, far from the madding crowd, high above the clouds, dwelling amidst the death-like loneliness of the rocks.

And now the others follow his example—get up, stretch themselves, examine the valley, take a few steps forward, and then with royal dignity all five make their way, a compact body, slowly and with sure step over the rocks.

CHAPTER XLII

A NIGHT IN THE OPEN

THE sun has already gone to rest down in the valley, but up here it is still coquetting and admiring itself in the manifold mirrors.

The markhor, meanwhile, continue their downward journey, stopping every now and then to gaze around before nibbling at the sparse grass and moss as they slip, climb, and spring from rock to rock, from crag to crag.

And now I can distinctly see the master-buck through the telescope. He seldom bends down to graze, and when he does so, only for a few seconds. Sharply he raises his proud head, and, motionless, stares in our direction. Then slowly, and with majestic, dignified mien, he follows the rest of the flock.

It grows darker and darker up here in the mountains, but there is nothing to be done—the markhor are still too far off to risk a shot. The shades of night come quickly once the sun has sunk to rest, and twilight soon throws a veil over the game, hiding them from our straining sight. The stars peep forth; outlines become indistinct and darkness envelops hill and valley, man and beast. There is nothing for it but to go to roost for to-day.

Just as the soldier, after the wear and tear of battle, still holding his gun and in readiness for a sudden alarm, goes to rest, so do we now stretch our weary limbs and lie down where we are. In complete silence we prepare our camp, such as it is, on the first dry rock we can find. I empty my thermos bottle, wrap myself in my puschtin, and lie down at once. But for a long time my eyes remain wide open.

Again and again in imagination I live through the last few impressive, never-to-be-forgotten hours. I see the white bucks climb down; I see them stop and gaze suspiciously round, sniffing up the wind. I watch them come nearer step by step, feel my pulse quicken, and hear my heart beating to suffocation. My blood still courses quickly through my veins at the thought of those magnificent creatures.

And thus day by day do they wander up hill and down dale, keeping the sun company in this wonderful world of lonely isolation. Nothing but rocks meets them on their daily sojourn, and only sunbeams bring them a word of friendly greeting from afar. But all the more brilliantly is their rocky table lighted up by stars at night.

I lie motionless on my stony mattress for fear of

disturbing their majesties' evening repast. So still is the night in these parts that I scarcely dare to breathe. If only they do not come too near or scent us on the breeze!

Hour by hour does the night get lighter, and the air becomes ever more rarefied. I begin to shiver, and my eyelids droop over tired eyes.

But what was that? Can I have heard aright?

A distant noise, as of falling stones, reaches my ear; but all is still again, if anything stiller than before, except for the snoring of the men.

What a brilliant, glimmering, star-bespangled sky! What a boundless world of flame and light stretches above us, unseen for the most part by us mortals accustomed now to sickly lamplight and to the world's cheap, artificial glare!

It needs a night spent up here amongst the lonely rocks to convince one of the majesty of reality. For all these starry eyes follow the fortunes of the earth with mathematical precision to-day as yesterday, and as in the beginning of all things. And they still jealously guard their secrets and riddles from us as they twinkle in the dark sky like wax lights on a Christmas tree.

"Stilly night, holy night!"

Why has the Almighty seen fit to make the night so much more beautiful than the day—and then ordained that it shall be the time of sleep, of forgetfulness? The sun, on the other hand, shines on everyone and on everything, lighting up the ugliest corners of the earth in an unpoetical glare.

How different are the stars! They do not shine on the commonplace, prosaic things of this world, but veil themselves from the glance of the profane, and send their sweet light to charm the devout and thoughtful worshipper at their shrine. Lovingly light and shade are blended, the earth is veiled, and the heavens alone shine forth in purity and beauty.

One never feels lonely in the night. I love it and feel at home in it. I love it with all my senses—with my eyes, which see its beauty; with my ears, which hear its stillness; with my heart, which feels its friendliness. But the stars must shine, shine bright and clear, else the night is black and drear as death.

Thank God, they are shining above me now as they sail about in all their glory on the dark blue ocean!

CHAPTER XLIII

AN UNSUCCESSFUL CHASE

LITTLE by little the stars grow paler as they make room for the sun.

We are prepared to shoot at any moment. Night's curtain rises ever higher, and things in the foreground become quite distinct in the full light of day, but not a sign of markhor anywhere to be seen.

Only yesterday we watched them grazing so peacefully, utterly without suspicion, on the opposite hillside; and to-day the spot is deserted, the world seems empty for as far as we can see through our glasses.

"The Sahib ought to have had a shot at them yesterday evening. They were not too far off, and it was not too dark."

As a matter of fact I had already raised my rifle and was on the point of pulling the trigger, but my heart was beating so hard that the sight was not steady enough and I dared not shoot.

Was it the dark veil of evening that dimmed my eyes, or was I dazzled at the sight of those almost supernatural creatures? Or did I hear the warning voice of the white nuns of Baumbach's "Zlatarog"?

I know not the reason. I only know I could not shoot.

"Don't be afraid, you will all get your backshish just the same."

Willingly will I pay it, if only in memory of yesterday. Why should I shoot into uncertainty? One single report and the poetry of the valley is gone. Off go the markhor—for ever, as far as I am concerned, and only rocks and stones remain behind.

And now Samdu believes he can descry an ibex in the far distance high above us amongst some snowy, projecting rocks. After a careful examination through our glasses we have to admit that he is right, and very soon we see a second, and a third, and a fourth. But miles and miles separate us from them—miles of chasms, precipices, and ravines insurmountable for the human foot. And it is not long before we lose sight of them even through the telescope, as they climb ever higher towards the heavens. They must have got wind of us in the night and have now left this nullah for the present.

What a bitter disappointment!

CHAPTER XLIV

FOLLOWING UP THE MARKHOR

Five long days, and not one glimpse at a markhor!

Unceasingly we have climbed from rock to rock, watching, waiting, freezing—all in vain!

Paul sends me a message: "Ram Sheik is going to kill Lali to-morrow. He is the last of the sheep."

I had quite forgotten poor Lali—how quickly we human beings forget! But now I again begin to think about the poor old sheep that had been a good friend to me up here in the lonely mountains.

One must observe animals with the heart, looking deep down into their eyes; thus only can one read their life-story and cull stores of knowledge from their depths.

"Certainly not! I forbid it! I would rather go hungry! Lali's life must be spared! Wring the necks of all the chickens, but don't touch the red sheep!"

Egoism again!

Have not the poor chickens also warm blood in their veins?

RAM SHEIK COOKS UNDER DIFFICULTIES, WHILST PAUL SUPERINTENDS.

CHAPTER XLV

STORMY WEATHER

AND even if I never succeed in getting a markhor, and get instead a cold which will last me all my life, I shall never regret all the troubles and privations and dangers of the last ten days. For how indescribably glorious is God's world up here! What an unearthly picture it presents!

I pray with my eyes and see with my heart!

God created these mountains, these great cathedrals of the world, and He has furnished them with His own treasures—pillars of rock, altars of snow, the blue sky as cupola, and choirs of stones and pebbles.

The plains where we men live cannot compare with them, be they never so lovely. And art, however perfect, cannot be mentioned in the same breath.

For miles and miles, far away into the horizon, they stretch their silvery expanse. Here primeval rocks shed their costliest blossoms, of a gigantic size and sparkling like stars. They are whiter than the loveliest garden lilies, glimmering like pearls in the light of heaven, turning to blood-red rubies in the sun's crimson rays, and blacker than jet when the storm-clouds gather. Man may make posies and garlands of all other flowers, but these mountain blossoms he cannot even hold in his hand!

What do Mars and Venus matter to these royal stones?

What a pigmy I feel—I, a man of average height, of the Teutonic race! One's insignificance comes home to one very clearly up here, and that God, so often forgotten in towns and churches, seems very near. With every breath one draws, one's soul seems to expand and grow.

I am filled with astonishment, wonder, and awe for the Mighty Hand that has modelled these rocks and given them their insignia of grandeur.

CHAPTER XLVI

THE MARKHOR SEEM TO HAVE DISAPPEARED

THE days follow one another slowly and are all very much alike. We climb and sway, wrestle and tussle, fall and pick ourselves up—all to no purpose! We melt beneath the sun's glowing rays by day, only to freeze beneath the cold rocks, near poor fires, by night.

"I'll hold out for another two days, but after that we start the retreat."

Two coolies bring us fresh provisions.

Paul writes: "We really must kill the red sheep. The new batch of supplies from Uri has not turned up. All the chickens are dead, and even the rice and flour for Count Sahib are coming to an end."

"How you must have stuffed yourselves down there! Wretched cook!"

Ram Sheik, of course, half-Christian, half-Hindu, had the key of the store-room. And now the poor sheep must suffer for his sins!

"I shall be down by the 25th, and Lali is to remain alive till I come! This is my will and the will of Allah!"

The bearers swear and declare that they have seen fresh tracks of markhor. But then they will swear to anything for the sake of backshish. Let them guide us to-morrow morning. We shall not be able to stay up here much longer anyhow, for the black clouds are already gathering together in the south.

The air has lost its transparency, and the sky is getting more and more sickly-looking. Fantastically-shaped clouds hurry hither and thither. They are the forerunners of the summer south-western monsoon, which, in the middle of June, starts upon its long dark journey from the equator across the Indian Ocean, breaking up the smooth surface of the latter into mighty waves, seething cauldrons, and foam-flecked breakers—a black sea dotted with white lights. Roars of thunder, flashes of lightning follow one another unceasingly, till it seems as if the end of the world has come, and for three months rain pours down in torrents on to the peninsula. Nothing can stop the monsoon's dreary march until it reaches the highest points of the Himalayas, and then it is forced to halt before those rocky barriers, and, whether it will or no, bring its damp journey to an end.

The sun, which had for so long poured its comforting rays upon us, sank to rest behind a grey veil, and now the stars are hidden from time to time by clouds marching like a funeral procession across the sky.

Everything has changed quite suddenly—the mountains, the air, Nature's whole mood, and ours too.

CHAPTER XLVII

MY FIRST SHOT AT A MARKHOR

THE night was pitch black, and the morning dawns dull and grey. Wrapped in mist, the new-born day begins its round of work.

The bearers were right after all. There are certainly fresh tracks of the markhor to be seen. We follow them carefully. They lead us up a steep incline and hurry us over the frozen snow—where they lead, we must follow.

With untiring zeal the shikaris scoop out one foothold after the other, and step by step we climb upwards. From time to time loose stones and lumps of ice fall with a clatter into the depths below.

Why must the markhor choose this particular route!

Dull peals of thunder come from afar, and brilliant flashes of lightning make the dark day light. From time to time puffs of wind scatter the mist, driving it from rock to rock. Intermittent sunbeams are sharply eclipsed by angry clouds. Every now and then a momentary pause occurs, reminding one of a feverish pulse. It is quite mild, but not at all hot, and yet we perspire tremendously.

Trusting entirely to the sure foothold and experience of the stalkers, I let their athletic muscles bear the full burden of my weight.

Far below me yawns the precipice. One false step and it will prove my grave. But a beautiful grave, for one would lie softly on pure white sheets, beneath gigantic memorial stones placed there by Nature, the greatest of sculptors.

Again and again my glance is drawn to the depths below, only to return and wander again to the far distance—a landscape of incomparable beauty, giving the impression of an ocean whipped into fury by a storm, and suddenly petrified. Over all spreads a delicate violet shade, beneath a steel-grey sky.

"Take care, Sahib, ice!" whispers Sultana.

I hold on to him tighter than ever, and he pulls me over.

Safe once more, my eye wanders in search of markhor tracks, utterly regardless of steep and slippery heights. Poetry and prose, joy and anxiety, follow one another in quick succession.

My mountain pilots, insensible to either, go steadily on. Their whole life is a poem of heroism. Every hour has its dangers; daring is their duty, adventure an everyday, necessary element of their calling. Their faces are full of energy, and they seldom smile.

Thank God, we are up at last! There is only a man's height still to climb, and then we shall be able to look over.

The shikaris hand me my rifle, the cartridges, and the telescope. I screw it on and load.

"Stop a minute. I must get my breath." Very carefully, and almost with affection, the men scoop out the last few steps.

"We think the game must be quite near, the tracks are so very fresh. It would be best if the Sahib would go up and have a look round alone first."

Off with the toupee! Higher and higher, inch by inch, my head goes slowly and carefully up. And before I can look over I hear a sharp hiss, and at the same moment a short, broken-off bark—the first sound in these mountains. It seems half ghostly, half reproachful. "Got you, you thief, you disturber of the peace."

"Markhor," whisper the shikaris.

I wriggle onward on my stomach, peep over, wriggle still further, lean over still more, and yet for the life of me I can see nothing. Where on earth did the hissing note of warning come from? It seemed to be so near. They ought to be standing directly beneath me. Questioningly I turn towards the men, who are squatting on a lower level, and as I do so my eyes rest suddenly on that which they have been so hungrily seeking, standing in a dark fissure, free from snow, about fifty feet off.

There they stand, as if turned to stone, grey against grey, of a gigantic size, with their heads raised, long, knotted beards hanging from their necks, and horns of a majestic length spreading upwards — like creatures from another world. Without a sound, motionless as marble, with a stillness as of death they stare at me.

There are five of them.

Up goes my rifle as quick as lightning, and steadily taking aim, I shoot at the front one.

He falls and lies like a log, whilst the others trundle down the mountain-side in lumbering bounds.

And now, at last, I am able to distinguish the master-buck. His horns are much longer and wider apart, his neck is much broader, and his beard thicker and longer than the others.

He takes the lead. I follow him with my rifle, aim with deliberation, shoot. But without making a sign the buck continues his journey.

"A miss," whisper the shikaris.

"In Allah's name, Sahib, shoot again," they croak out the next moment, and there, before our eyes, in full sight, stands the first buck as large as life, and before I can re-load he has slowly taken cover behind some rocks.

"He will lie down again in a minute," says Sultana comfortingly. "Be careful, Sahib; we've got plenty of time," and so saying he prevents me from hurrying thoughtlessly on. "The rocks are sharp and slippery; the Sahib could easily fall. Besides, it is better to leave the buck time to get more ill, to be obliged to lie down."

We load both guns as quickly as possible.

"How could I have been so foolish and careless as to have forgotten to load the second one before!"

We go to the spot where my first shot fell, but there is no blood to be seen.

The tracks lead sheer downwards. We follow, and notice that they get slower, and then they are lost on some snowless rocks.

"Take care," beg the shikaris.

These rolling stones are not to be trusted. Snow and earth can come crashing down at any moment. Pebbles and shingle roll past continually—messengers of a possible landslip. Death and destruction follow in their train.

We clamber down the steep ridge—no matter how steep it is, the wounded buck helps us to bear everything.

"Only get on, get on; I must have him."

In vain we look into every crevice, hunt about in every hiding-place. For a long time in vain, and then at last the quarry shows himself. But he is already much further off than we had expected. We can see him about four hundred yards in front of us, standing on a slope split into many gorges.

"He must be very ill, or he would look towards us and would not stand still."

Slowly he continues his rocky journey, but soon he stops suddenly and begins to wind his way down towards the valley. And now I shoot.

The stones beneath the animal are scattered hither and thither; but he himself stands motionless. Before, however, I can shoot a second time he starts again, slowly winding his way from rock to rock. My gun follows him, and the moment he stands still I shoot.

"Too high this time." And in hurried leaps the markhor disappears—for ever!

CHAPTER XLVIII

THINGS LOOK BAD

Gladly could I have committed suicide at that moment!

"Bara, bara markhor," moan the shikaris, as they show their disappointment with many gesticulations. I try hard to justify myself.

"It was all too sudden, too unexpected, too near. Only fifty feet off. My telescope was set for seventy-five yards. I forgot to aim lower, aimed instead straight at the shoulder, and in that way I only scratched him; he was only stunned, and is no more wounded than I am."

All hope is gone; the markhor have disappeared for ever, at all events so far as I am concerned. All this shooting has driven them away for weeks to come.

In vain all our work, our efforts, our trouble, our hardships, and all the expense. In vain—what a wretched, cheerless word!

And I was so sure I had killed him, felt so triumphant, and had even counted on a double shot!

10

And now the long journey back over the rocks without the courage hope gives in one's heart and in one's legs.

I sat still a little longer, and then we started on our backward march, but much more slowly than I had come. More in the arms of my men than on my own legs, I at last managed to reach the point at which this drama had begun. There we had left Unkar with breakfast and warm coats.

His eyes asked questions, and I felt his reproaches. He began a lively conversation with his comrades —about me, of course, and my clumsiness—but I could only understand "markhor, markhor." How I hated the word! For me it meant only reproach, scorn, mockery, and disappointment.

These Zlatarogs, too, must be under the protection of the white nuns, and nothing but scorn and despair can await him who is bold enough to dare to set foot in their mountain paradise!

"I suppose you think you can get him down with that thing," I grumble disagreeably, as the three shikaris continually direct the telescope towards the spot where the sick beast was supposed to be.

"Bas."

"Markhor," whispers Sultana, pointing across the chasm.

"For goodness' sake don't let me hear that word again—bas, for everlasting bas. Enough of this cruel game!"

"Markhor, Sahib," whispers the man again beseechingly, pointing in the same direction and handing me the telescope.

In the far distance, high up in the snow, far away, I can actually see a markhor. What's the good of him to me? Ah, now he is leaving the pass! And at once he is followed by a second, a third, a fourth.

"There were five bucks. Where is the last? So he has had to stop behind after all, too ill to go with the rest—perhaps we may still hope to find him."

The men's sad faces also light up quite suddenly. We understand each other. What an event! They are smiling. "It will be hard work looking for him, Sahib, but we'll bring you the markhor with Allah's help!"

CHAPTER XLIX

NOWHERE TO BE FOUND

THE shikaris take a shorter way this time to arrive at the point where we gave up the search.

Samdu and Unkar, well acquainted with the locality, form the van ; Sultana and a bearer accompany me.

Strong with hope, but very slowly, we begin our climb over the rocks. We can all feel our bones, for it had been a hard day's work already.

A cold drizzle was falling, and now and then snowflakes floated through the air.

Up and down, slowly and with difficulty, but always onwards, our journey continues. But our goal is still far away.

A deathly stillness reigns in the mountains.

"What was that ?"

A sudden deafening roar makes the air tremble, splits my ear.

Has one of the leading shikaris fallen down a precipice ?

Sultana and the bearer stand still and listen.

Broken sounds reach us from below; they go on and on and never seem to stop.

Sultana shouts as well, and soon the bearer adds his voice to the noise.

How Indian! If the master gives a quiet order, everyone begins to shout the same, from the highest to the lowest, and the last shouts the loudest.

Loud but indistinct noises answer us from below.

Ah, at last I can hear two voices quite distinctly! Thank God they are both alive! But what on earth can have happened to them?

"What's the matter, Sultana? Explain! Quick!"

He falls at my feet, clasps me round the knees, kisses my hands, stares at me, is struck dumb.

"For God's sake, what has happened? Tell me at once!"

"Markhor, markhor!" he bursts out at last, shouting and rejoicing with all his might.

"Markhor!" roars the bearer in my ear, and he also falls down before me.

"Markhor!" they shout from down below.

Has a miracle taken place? How is it possible? Can the wounded creature have turned off here?

"Have we really got him, Sultana? Is he dead?"

"Yes, Sahib, bara markhor. It is the biggest one—the one the Sahib shot at the second time. He ran in this direction, but we forgot him in our hunt after the wounded one."

CHAPTER L

THE FALL OF THE INDIAN ZLATAROG

Excitement lends us wings—we fly down!

There he lies.

I draw nearer and look in respectful silence at his beautiful horns, his splendid beard, and his strongly-built body in its rough, silvery coat.

On white sheets he lies—this Indian Zlatarog. His coffin is ornamented with stones and purple-coloured flowers—triglavroses!

His body is still warm, but he lies motionless in death's rigidity, for life has already left him—life that is so rare amongst these mountains. The king of the rocks is dead!

Black clouds begin to gather overhead, the air becomes cold, uncannily roars the wind.

Once more the sun breaks through to kiss his darling who has so often followed him over hill and dale; blossoms of silver he scatters on the grave and then makes haste to be gone.

The mountains drape themselves in 'mourning

garments and the rocks and stones add their lamentations.

Flashes of lightning scurry across the sky and torrents of tears stream down. The hills, the rocks, the stones weep loudly, and a voice of thunder vibrates through the ever-silent world.

Once again has mankind slaughtered!

"Triglavroses, triglavroses!"